NEW CASTROL BOOK of CAR CARE

ABCDE 212
FGHIJ
KLMNO
PQ!

HAYNES

New CASTROL BOOK of CAR CARE

Published and distributed by J H Haynes & Company Limited, of
Sparkford, Yeovil, Somerset BA22 7JJ for
Castrol Limited of Burmah House, Pipers Way, Swindon SN3 1RE

This is a completely new edition of the well known
Castrol handbook, following *CAR CARE* and *The Castrol Book
of CAR CARE.*
New CASTROL BOOK of CAR CARE.   August 1974

ISBN 085696 212 0

Text Brian Chalmers-Hunt
Illustration Terry Davey
Editorial Production Tim Parker

Made in England by J H Haynes & Company Limited
Sparkford, Yeovil, Somerset BA22 7JJ

Contents

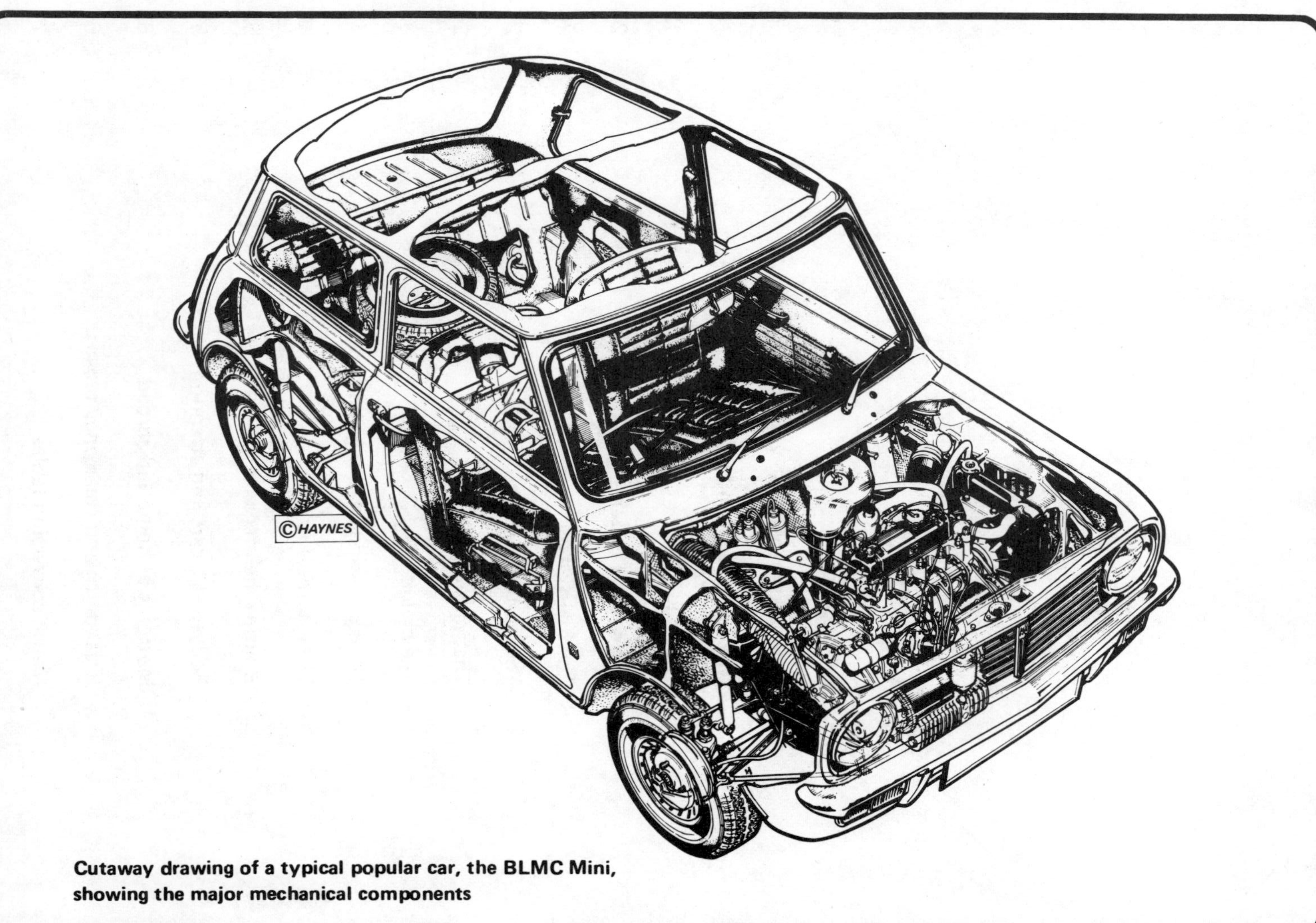

Cutaway drawing of a typical popular car, the BLMC Mini, showing the major mechanical components

Introduction

The aim of this book is to explain in a simple language the basic principle of how a motor car works, why it runs and what needs to be done to ensure that it keeps working in the way that it was designed to.

It is not meant to replace the owner's handbook as supplied by the car manufacturer but rather to supplement it, by providing a background for the beginner and by clarifying some points for the more experienced.

Although each car is individually very complicated there are obviously certain basic essentials common to all and it is these that have been described in the following chapters.

A happy partnership - you and your car

There is no advice more likely to ruin a car than 'If it's working, well leave it alone'.

Of course it is true that continuous fiddling is unlikely to be good for any mechanical device, planned maintenance is the only way to go, to ensure that your car will give long reliable service.

Whilst it is usual to complain about the lack of reliability of a car, remember that if it were 99.9% efficient there could still be some ten to twenty items to go wrong at any one time! There are moving parts which wear, electrical parts which age, and the body panels which corrode. Looking at it this way it does seem that it is a losing battle from the start.

Regrettably this may be true. All cars have a useful life, but just how long and useful that life is will depend to a great extent upon the amount of proper and regular attention that is given to the car.

One important thing to remember is that 'care cuts costs'. As well as reducing wear and incorrect running, regular maintenance and checking of parts before they actually fail can give enough warning to enable adjustment or partial replacement to effect a complete cure. Waiting for the inevitable normally means a complete overhaul or a replacement unit.

Breakdowns rarely occur in a warm garage at home and at a convenient time. By the side of a motorway or on a cold wet night is a much more usual site for trouble to strike. Unfortunately there is no way of making your car completely foolproof against breakdown, but there is one way of minimising the risk - regular care and attention. It is often forgotten that the motor car is a highly complex engineering device which baffles many average car owners - and sometimes the experts as well. Treat it well and it will look after you.

There are ways in which the motorist who is not particularly interested in technicalities can contribute to the smooth running of his car, without necessarily performing any maintenance work himself. In addition, the ability to recognise and diagnose faults may save costly repair bills.

Fuel

The premium grade petrols are worth the extra few pence, especially if your engine has a moderately high compression ratio, and it may be advantageous to have the carburettor adjusted to suit a particular brand and to stick to that brand thereafter. It is not worth the extra expense of using a 100 octane petrol if your engine is not designed with a suitably high compression ratio.

Running-in

When a new or reconditioned engine is installed in a car, its moving parts have a certain degree of surface roughness which must be smoothed down before the engine can be driven safely on full load. In order to ensure a perfect fit when the smoothing down process is complete, bearing surfaces are assembled on the tight side and if the engine is overstressed early in its life there is a danger that seizure may occur and cause permanent damage.

The latest recommendation for running-in concerns not so much the following of a rigid speed schedule as the need to prevent the engine 'slogging'. This is simply achieved by maintaining a light touch on the accelerator pedal, the avoiding of fierce acceleration and the changing to a lower gear immediately it is felt that the engine is beginning to labour.

Fuel economy

Nowadays most motorists are interested in maximum fuel economy and it is generally appreciated that the most significant factor in

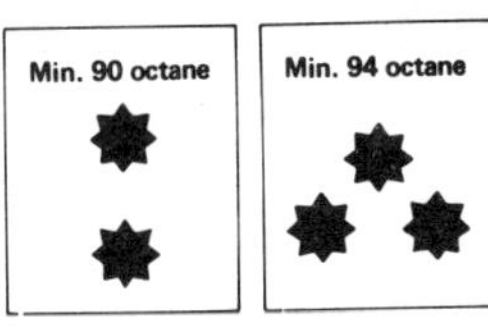

Octane rating symbols. Use the correct one for your car

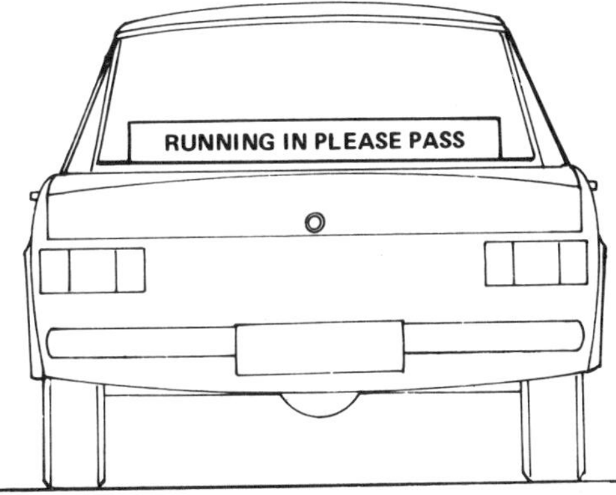

Tell others you are running-in, even with a re-conditioned engine

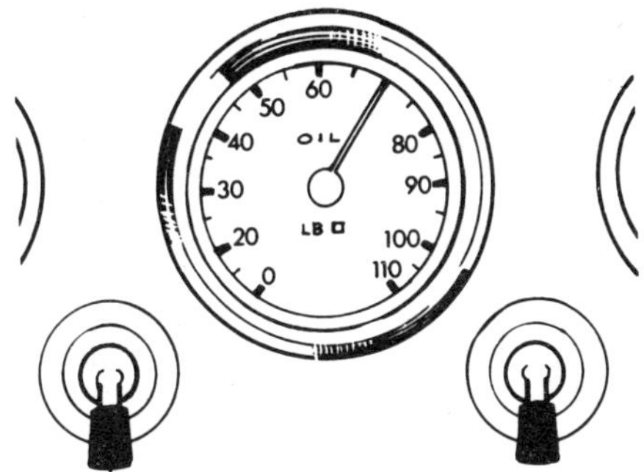

'Oil pressure tells the best story'
If your car is fitted with an oil pressure gauge you will have a useful guide to engine wear. High pressures can be just as damaging as low pressures, so check with your handbook or local agent to see what the correct pressure range should be

determining petrol consumption is speed. It has been proved over and over again that petrol is consumed at a minimum rate when the speed is between 35 to 40 mph. This means that petrol consumption is increased if the car is driven slowly or at a greater speed than 40 mph. This is because wind resistance becomes far more significant and increases in a much greater ratio than the increase in speed. Additionally the petrol/air mixture supplied to the engine by the carburettor increases in richness as the throttle is opened beyond the half way point.

Economy can be obtained by driving the car in a gentle manner and this includes, besides restricting speed to about 40 mph, the avoidance of rapid acceleration and maximum utilisation of the top gear. By looking well ahead, the throttle can be eased back earlier than normal so avoiding excessive use of the brakes.

The warming-up period of an engine can be considerably reduced by the use of a radiator blind especially on short journeys.

Ensure that the various engine settings are correctly adjusted and to minimise tyre rolling drag the pressures can be raised by 2-3 lb/sq in. The brakes should be checked to ensure that they are not binding and the front wheel (and in some cases rear wheel) alignment is correct.

Starting the engine

A routine should be developed to check the various controls and instruments before and during initial starting of the engine much in the same way as an airline pilot before take-off. The following points should be observed:

1 Check that the handbrake is on and the gear lever (or selector) is in neutral.

2 Switch on the ignition and ensure that red ignition warning light is glowing indicating that the battery is not being charged. When an ammeter is fitted this will show a small discharge. If an electric fuel pump supplies petrol to the carburettor it may be heard to tick a few times and stop. When an oil pressure gauge is fitted it should show a zero reading or a green light will glow to indicate no pressure. Be careful, however, because on some cars this light appears when oil pressure is satisfactory and goes out at low or zero pressure so check this point carefully. The fuel gauge should show petrol in the tank.

3 If cold pull out the choke, start the engine and the red ignition warning light should go out. The ammeter should show a charge reading which will increase as the engine is speeded up. If a low reading is maintained it is usually an indication that the battery is in a good state of charge.

4 The oil pressure gauge should now give a reading of about 25 lb/in^2 or higher although the actual reading will depend on the engine, grade of oil, and temperature of the oil and engine speed. The oil pressure warning light will go out or glow depending on which system is used.

Of all instruments that can be fitted the oil pressure gauge is the most important as far as engine care goes and should be under constant observation of the driver, not only during initial starting but during subsequent driving. If the reading disappears or the warning light indicates loss of pressure stop at once and investigate.

5 The water temperature gauge is an instrument which is not fitted to all cars but it is of real value as it indicates the engine running temperature. This is particularly important for the motorist who uses his car for short journeys only. Under these conditions the engine has rarely had time to warm up and therefore does not run at its best efficiency. A cold running engine will wear more rapidly than an engine running at normal operating temperature.

6 Allow the engine to idle for a few minutes not forgetting to push in the choke control as soon as possible and the car is ready to be driven away.

To summarise

Starting Starting from cold is the most critical time for an engine from the point of view of wear. The oil will have drained from all the working surfaces, so during the first few revolutions only a thin residual film of oil will be acting as the lubricant. This has to suffice until the pump can fill the oilways and replenish the bearing surfaces. The 'thinner' the oil the easier this is, which is why it is important to use a multi-grade oil such as Castrol GTX, which remains free flowing at low temperatures, helping to reduce 'cold start' wear to a minimum.

Use of the choke The choke alters the fuel/air ratio to give a petrol-rich mixture for easy starting. However, when the engine is cold the petrol is likely to condense on the cylinder walls and wash off the residual oil film; and if the choke is left out for too long an appreciable amount of petrol can accumulate in the sump and dilute the oil. The golden rule with the choke is, 'use it as little as possible'.

Warming up Once started, an engine should be brought to its normal operating temperature as soon as possible. The engine should not be allowed to tick over for any length of time while cold and neither should it be accelerated fiercely to high speeds. Moderate speed and gentle acceleration should be used until the engine is hot.

Start/stop driving Many motorists use their cars largely for start/stop driving - in other words, they drive for only very short distances between lengthy stops, such as going shopping or driving to the station. This type of driving is very hard on a car because the engine seldom has time to reach its correct operating temperature and is therefore running cold most of the time. These conditions cause the oxidation-inhibitor and dispersant additives to be depleted much more quickly than usual, leading to rapid and heavy contamination of the lubricant. The only solution is to change the oil much more frequently, as recommended by most car manufacturers in their handbooks.

Normal driving Normal driving is usually understood to consist of starting the car and driving off with the minimum of fuss and loitering, and then cruising at an even speed well within the car's capabilities. Driven in this way a car engine is capable of achieving very high mileages with very little wear.

Why lubrication and servicing?

Whenever two surfaces rub together, say a tyre on the road, there is friction between them. If there was not, the car would not run at all, as it is only the friction between the tyre treads and the road surface that enables the motive force of the engine to move the car along and then for the friction between the brake linings and drums or discs which stop the car moving. The trouble is that friction is not only present where it is wanted but it also appears where it is not wanted - in every moving part of the car. Friction always means wear.

When two bare metal surfaces are rubbed together there is a high rate of wear which increases with the pressure exerted on the contact area and the relative speed of the two surfaces.

Friction also produces heat. This can be enough to raise the surface temperature to a point where the metals melt and become welded together. This is what happens when an engine 'seizes-up'. Preventing friction and all the problems that come with it, is where the principle of lubrication comes in.

The only way to minimise friction and wear is to prevent the two surfaces concerned from actually touching, by the introduction of a slipping layer between them. This layer can be grease, oil or plastic. Every contact area has its own peculiar problems which will be dealt with in later chapters. For example, the oil film between the piston rings and the cylinder bore, working in the 'worst' conditions of high speed and at a high temperature, has a rather different set of problems compared with those of the grease layer in a suspension joint which is moving at a relatively low speed, but at a very high weight loading.

It is the car and lubricant manufacturer's job to ensure, through research and development that the correct lubricant is applied to all moving surfaces. The owner's job is to ensure that through regular servicing, there is always enough of the correct lubricant in the right place to control friction, and therefore wear.

Modern motor cars need very little servicing, technology has now reduced the number of points that need attention, and the frequency of servicing has been reduced to once every three or six months. This has been brought about by great improvements not only in lubrication techniques but also in metal coating development. Where every steering and suspension joint was once a steel ball riding in a steel cup, or a steel pin in a metal tube, advances in plastics design have enabled the bearing surfaces to be coated with nylon, PTFE or similar substances to produce a very low friction joint.

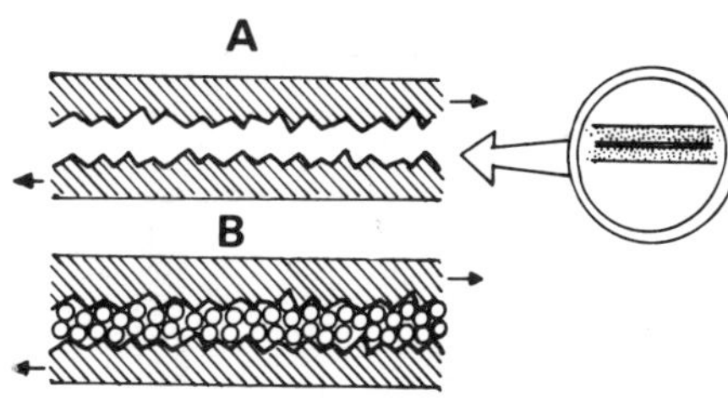

Friction and lubrication
a) Though a piece of metal may appear to have a smooth surface, when viewed under a microscope it can be seen to be very rough
b) The only way to prevent two metal surfaces being damaged by the effects of friction is to introduce a layer of low friction material between them. Lubricating oil can provide this layer and protect both surfaces

Even where a straight metal to metal joint is used, modern greases are much more resistant to extremes of pressure, heat, water and salt.

Lubricating greases usually comprise of mineral oils mixed with substances which, chemically speaking, are called 'soaps'. These are selected to give the required high and low temperature performances so that the grease does not solidify at low temperatures nor melt at high temperatures. Additives are also included to prevent corrosion of the metal components.

The important thing to remember about all aspects of servicing is that parts may well carry-on working long after the recommended renewal periods, but they are then invariably working at well below their best and may well cause rapid deterioration of supplementary parts. Just because recommended servicing times are far apart does not mean they can be ignored - quite the reverse. When service times are reached, the items listed by the manufacturers as due for renewal can be expected to have come to the end of their most efficient life. To ensure that full benefit of maximum protection is obtained, always follow the recommended servicing schedule and ensure that the correct grades of oils and greases are used.

The service intervals advised by the manufacturer are based on the use of lubricants which they recommend. Before any lubricant is sanctioned, it is put through some very stringent tests.

It might be safe to use pre-war quality lubricants provided that the same pre-war service intervals were followed but most motorists would not like to grease the suspension joints once a week!

Modern car engines are very highly stressed and run at high engine revolutions, giving power outputs that many a pre-war sports car owner would be proud of. It is not only advances in engine design that enables this to be done, but without high quality engine oils the mechanical components would very quickly fail under the strain. Buying anything other than the best is a false economy as far as engine oils are concerned.

It must also be emphasised that the oil change periods quoted in the handbook supplied by the car manufacturer apply only for motoring under favourable conditions - regular long distance runs on good roads in good weather.

The different packages in which oil, grease and additives are sold help to identify them

Even given good roads and passable weather, most motoring consists of comparatively short, town journeys which do not give the engine time to reach its ideal operating temperature. Under such conditions, car manufacturers recommend that the oil is changed twice as often. Initially this will cost the motorist more but will be more than repaid in longer engine life.

There are many other items requiring routine servicing which will be covered in this book as each section of the car is dealt with, but basically the same principle applies whatever model of car the reader owns. Contact breaker points in the distributor, spark plugs, air filter, brake fluid and all the other items recommended by the manufacturers for changing at regular intervals will still continue to function, long after their basic cycle has finished, but don't forget that they will be working with ever decreasing efficiency and always be potential sources of trouble. Really neglect them and before long they will cause a breakdown, by which time they may well have damaged other allied components as well.

Those car owners who carry out their own maintenance can easily keep a careful check on intervals between services and the materials used, but many owners have to rely on the skill of their local garage.

Despite the constant stream of anti-garage publicity, the majority of garages do try to take proper care of their customer's cars and a great deal can be gained by showing an obvious interest in your car and assisting the garage. Before the car goes in for servicing, read the handbook and see exactly what has to be done to the car. There is nothing to be gained by complaining to the garage that they failed to do a certain job, if they were told to carry out a manufacturer's recommended service which did not include that particular job in the first place. Never rely on the Reception Engineer's memory - give the garage precise written instructions of the work wanted.

This will eliminate any chance of items being forgotten and in the event of jobs not being done, a record of exact instructions is available. If trouble is experienced complain to the owner or manager of the garage. It's his livelihood which depends on keeping customers. The best way of building up a good relationship with a

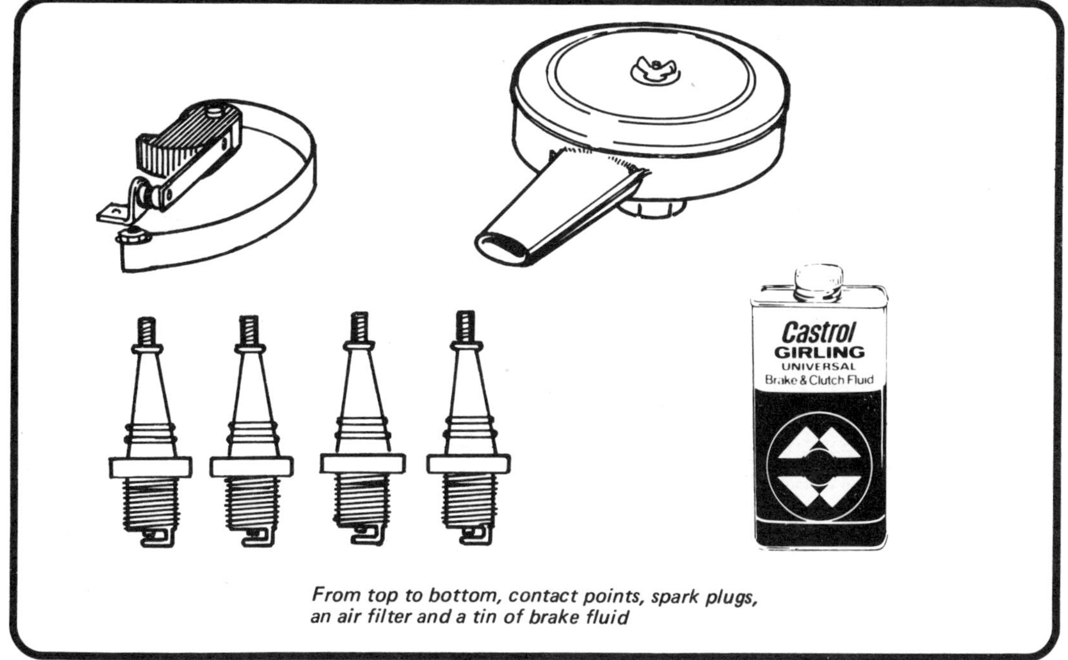

From top to bottom, contact points, spark plugs, an air filter and a tin of brake fluid

garage is to avoid misunderstanding and to try to help them. Make sure appointments are kept on time, consideration works both ways.

If the car has been owned since new its service history will obviously be known, but if a secondhand car has been purchased it is always best to play safe and assume that it has never been serviced. Using the car manufactuer's handbook or applicable Castrol Service Chart, have the work done systematically right through the service list undertaken either by yourself or your garage. Go round every grease point and pump in grease until all the old grease has been expelled. Inspect all the brake linings and/or pads for wear, cleaning out all the old dust and inspecting the drums or discs for scoring and the master and wheel cylinders for any signs of leakage.

Change all the oils and filters. Even though they may look clean, there will probably be no record as to what grade or make of oil has been used, so be safe and change it. Similarly go through the rest of the service list, change the spark plugs and contact breaker points, cleaning and adjusting the carburettor, renewing the air filter element etc.

Only by checking every item on the list can one be sure that individual parts are up to the job required and not overdue for renewal. This also gives a starting point from which the new owner may begin the routine servicing schedule.

A wise precaution is to purchase a car only from a dealer offering a guarantee including labour charges. These dealers are usually willing to certify that the car has received a full service and safety check before delivery to the new owner. This will, of course, be reflected in the purchase price but will represent a worthwhile-purchase.

An intending purchaser of an older and cheaper motor car with no mechanical knowledge would also find an evening course in car maintenance a helpful preliminary precaution. These are provided at a nominal charge by most local education authorities and details are usually available at Public Libraries.

When buying a used car look for the guarantee

A typical workshop manual, driver's handbook and Castrol Service chart

The engine

To move anything some form of effort or power is required. In a motor car this is needed chiefly to overcome friction where various parts rub against one another, and to overcome wind resistance. To climb a hill requires even more power as does increasing the speed of the car.

Power can be produced in various ways. Cars have been driven by steam or electric motors but the general practice is to use an engine known as the internal combustion engine. This type of engine converts heat energy into mechanical energy - the heat being obtained from the burning of a petrol/air mixture in a combustion chamber.

In a car engine fresh air is mixed with petrol at a pre-determined ratio and passed into a confined space where it is compressed. The mixture is then ignited by a spark plug, it burns, and causes the air to expand with a force such that it can be converted into a rotary movement of such magnitude that it can drive the wheels of the car.

So that the energy created may be used efficiently the burning process and force of expansion must be controlled within fine limits.

The first thing needed is a tube which is closed at one end. This is known as a cylinder and it is in this that the petrol and air mixture is burned. A metal plug is able to slide freely in the cylinder and is known as the piston. It can be pushed downwards by the force of the gas expanding.

To convert this linear movement of the piston into a rotary movement it must be joined by a connecting rod to a crank, in this case a crankshaft.

One passage is needed for admitting a fresh petrol/air mixture into the combustion chamber and a second passage needed to let out the used gases. These passages are known as inlet and exhaust ports. To control the entry of the fresh petrol/air mixture and the removal of the used gases two valves are required. These are known as inlet and exhaust valves.

A spark plug is inserted in the top end of the cylinder and is able to ignite the fresh petrol/air mixture between the top of the piston and underside of the top of the cylinder, this area being known as the combustion chamber.

The opening and closing of the valves and the time the spark jumps across the spark plug electrode gap are accurately controlled to interact so it is possible to make the piston move up and down the cylinder bore over and over again.

The modern petrol engine can be divided into several assemblies and may be discribed as follows.

Cylinder block and crankcase

This is the largest part of the engine. The top half is known as the cylinder block and the lower half the crankcase. In most engines the cylinder block and crankcase are cast in one piece.

The cylinder block contains the cylinders and pistons whilst the crankcase contains the crankshaft and camshaft. Other auxiliary components such as the mechanical fuel pump and generator are often mounted on the side of this assembly.

The cylinders are very accurately formed tubes or bores and it is in these that the pistons are able to slide up and down.

The pistons are a very accurate yet free fit in the cylinder bores and each piston has a number of piston rings which fit into circular grooves machined in the piston. The piston rings are able to press outwards against the cylinder bore walls. The top rings are known as compression rings and their function is to prevent the burning petrol/air mixture escaping between the piston and cylinder walls. The remaining rings fitted below the compression rings are to control the oil supply to the upper parts of the piston so preventing an high oil

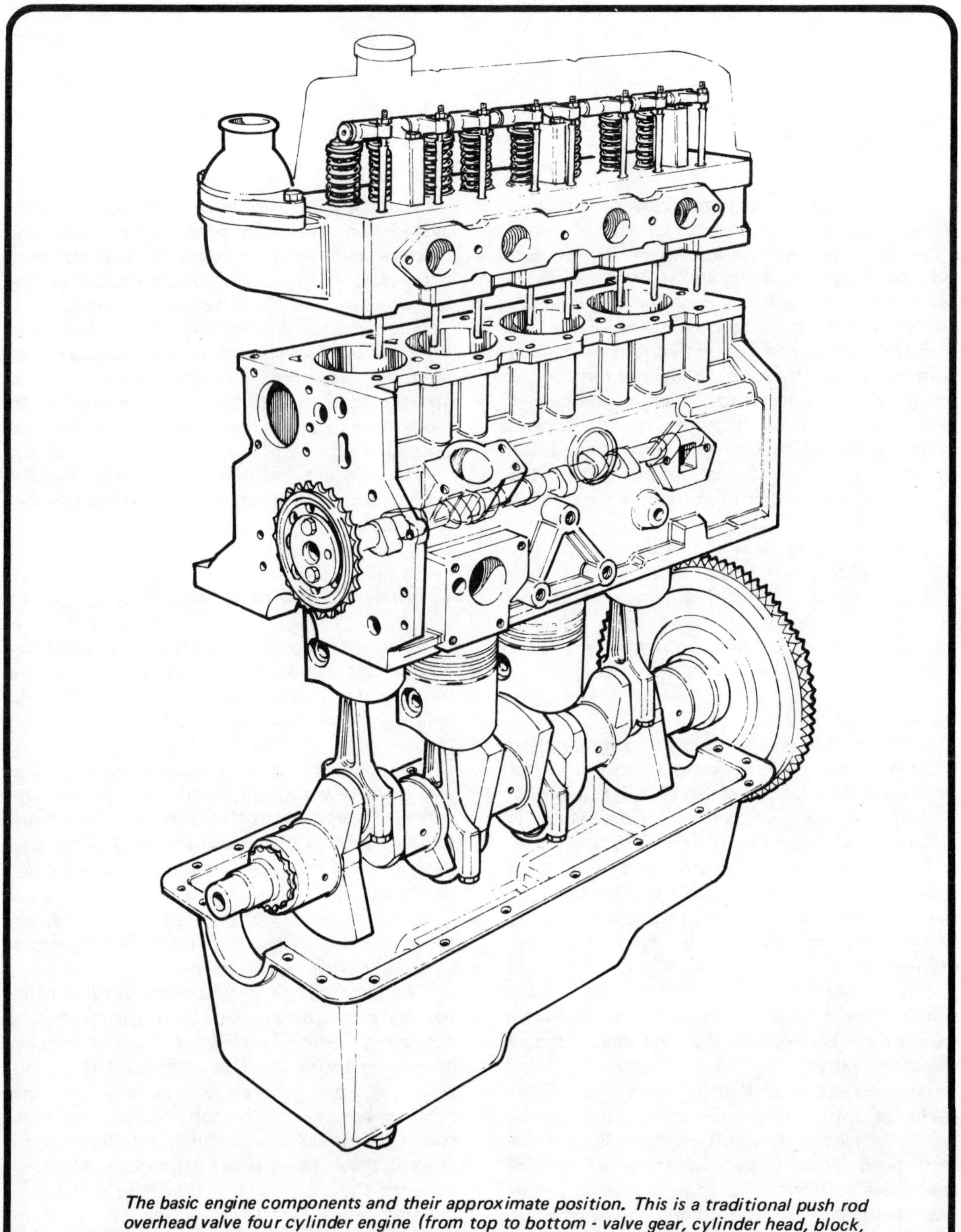

The basic engine components and their approximate position. This is a traditional push rod overhead valve four cylinder engine (from top to bottom - valve gear, cylinder head, block, camshaft, pistons, connecting rods, crankshaft, flywheel and sump)

consumption. These rings are known as oil control rings.

Each piston is joined to a connecting rod by means of a gudgeon pin which is fitted inside the piston and through the top or small end of the connecting rod.

The piston is 'attached' to the crankshaft by the connecting rod. The connecting rod runs on the crankshaft with a big-end bearing.

The bearing is usually a split (into two) shell bearing which 'wraps' around the crankshaft journal, and is held in place by a bolted cap.

The crankshaft is mounted in bearings known as main bearings in the crankcase.

At the rear end of the crankshaft is bolted a large heavy flywheel which is able to store energy and return the piston to the top of the bore after the burning gases have pushed it to the bottom of the bore. It also serves to ensure smooth running of the engine. Teeth are mounted on the circumference of the flywheel and are engaged by the pinion of the starter motor when first starting the engine.

The camshaft is mounted in bearings in the crankcase and has one cam for every valve. It is driven by the crankshaft by gears or chain and sprockets. As the cams rotate they operate cylindrical buckets called tappets which move pushrods to operate the valve gear.

A sheet metal pressing is bolted to the underside of the crankcase and its function is to hold the engine lubricating oil. It has a drain plug at its lowest part through which old oil may be drained out.

Cylinder head

The cylinder head is bolted to the top of the cylinder block. A gasket is used between these two parts to ensure a gas tight joint. It contains the inlet and exhaust valves, ports and spark plugs.

The inlet and exhaust ports are connected to the carburettor and exhaust system by passages in manifolds which are bolted to the side of the cylinder head.

Two valves are normally used for each cylinder; an inlet valve through which the fresh petrol/air mixture enters the cylinder and an exhaust valve through which the burnt gases pass into the exhaust pipe.

The valves are mounted in the ports and each is surrounded by one or two springs which keep it tightly closed except when it is opened by the valve gear.

The valve gear is bolted to the top of the cylinder head and comprises a rocker shaft, rockers and mountings. These rockers, one to each valve, are mounted on the rocker shaft so that one end of each rests on the top of a pushrod and the other end on the top of a valve stem.

There is a very small clearance between the valve stem and rocker tip to allow for expansion. Should this clearance not be correct the valve may not close completely causing leakage of the burning gases resulting in loss of engine power.

The valve gear is enclosed in a metal cover known as the rocker cover which is secured to the top of the cylinder head.

Most modern engines have both inlet and exhaust valves mounted in the cylinder head. This arrangement is known as an overhead valve (OHV) system. However, some earlier engines have both valves mounted in the cylinder block and in this instance they are known as side valve (SV). The latter arrangement is far simpler because there are less moving parts but it is difficult to position the valves in the best location for achieving maximum engine efficiency.

The camshaft is normally located in the crankcase but may be positioned on the top of the cylinder head. This type is known as an overhead camshaft (OHC).

Four Stroke cycle

Most car engines operate on what is known as the four stroke cycle, the figure overleaf shows the cycle in one cylinder.

Induction Stroke

The piston is at the top of the bore (tdc) and the inlet valve open. The exhaust valve is closed. The piston begins to descend and creates a partial vacuum in the cylinder; a fresh petrol/air mixture is drawn in through the open port. This downward movement is known as the Induction Stroke.

Compression Stroke

At the end of the induction stroke, the piston is now at the bottom of the bore (bdc) and the inlet valve closes. The crankshaft continues to revolve and pushes the piston upwards so that by the time it has reached top dead centre (tdc) all the gases contained in the cylinder have been squeezed up into the combustion space; thus at the end of the Compression Stroke the gas is under pressure (the degree of pressure relates to the compression ratio of the engine).

Power Stroke

The compressed gas is now ignited by an electric spark which jumps between the electrodes of the spark plug. The petrol vapour burns rapidly and heats up the air, which attempts to expand and creates high pressure on the top of the piston (crown). The resulting downward thrust of the piston is called the Power Stroke.

Exhaust Stroke

The piston having reached bottom dead centre (bdc) the exhaust valve is opened and during the following up-stroke the products of combustion are expelled through the exhaust port; this is the Exhaust Stroke. At the top of this stroke the exhaust valve closes and the engine then commences on the next complete cycle.

Note

In order to start this cycle of events it is necessary to rotate the engine by external means until at least one firing stroke has occured, after which, the energy stored up by the flywheel attached to the crankshaft keeps the engine rotating between power strokes. The engine then becomes self generating and the four stroke cycle is repeated in rapid succession. The four stroke cycle is completed in two complete revolutions of the crankshaft.

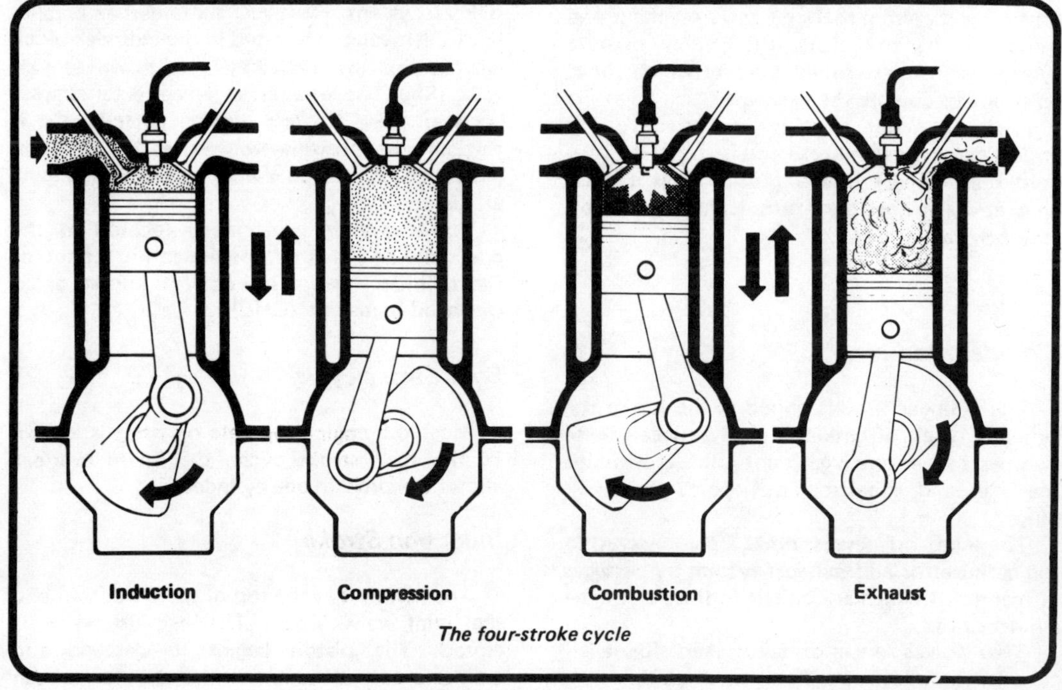

The four-stroke cycle

The two stroke engine

Although most car engines use the four stroke cycle some do in fact use the two stroke cycle which is more commonly used for motor cycles and scooters. The Wankel engine, another type of reciprocating engine, uses the four stroke principle.

The major difference between the two cycles is that, as with the four stroke cycle there is one power stroke every two revolutions of the crankshaft, with the two stroke cycle there is one power stroke every crankshaft revolution. This is far more acceptable for single cylinder engines, to ensure smooth running and even power output.

Engine lubrication

All the moving parts of an engine work at high temperatures and at high speed. The piston rings run against the walls of the cylinder bore, the crankshaft runs inside the main and big-end bearings, the crankshaft has to operate the valve mechanism and the valves run inside their guides. If all these surfaces were to run in metal-to-metal contact, friction and heat would soon destroy them.

Because all bearing surfaces are separated by a layer of engine oil there is no metal to metal contact.

The necessary oil is stored in the sump where it is picked up at a feed pipe and drawn by and into the oil pump. The oil leaves the pump under pressure and is fed through a filter into oil passages drilled in the cylinder block. These passages lead to the important parts in the block such as the crankshaft main bearings and camshaft bearings. The crankshaft itself also has oil passages drilled in it which are fed with oil under pressure at the main bearings. These passages carry oil through to the big-end bearings and out through the sides. This sprays oil into the piston and cylinder bore to keep a film of oil between the rings and the bore and therefore cool the piston. As more oil is sprayed in a continuous flow from the pump, the 'used' oil drops back into the sump to cool, and is then recirculated again.

As the oil travels through the various parts of the engine it may pick-up fragments of swarf and other loose particles which it carries through to the filter. The filter is a very, very fine sieve which will allow the oil to pass through but traps all the particles which could damage the engine if allowed to circulate.

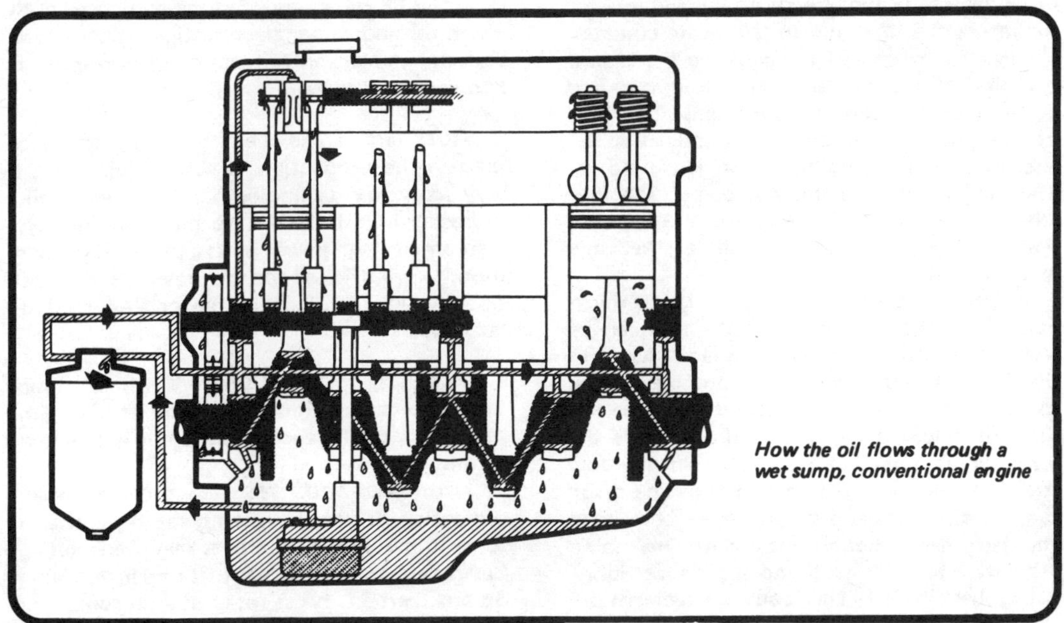

How the oil flows through a wet sump, conventional engine

This may sound straightforward enough but the oil has other demands to cope with which may not be immediately apparent. These are discussed below:

Viscosity   This is the term used to describe the thickness of the oil. There are light lubricating oils which can be as thin as petrol, and heavy gear oils which are thicker than some greases and have to be heated before they will pour at all. Viscosity is very much dependant on temperatures. The lubricating oil used in an engine gets hot in carrying out its secondary task of cooling the bearing surfaces and yet when cool it must be thin enough to be circulated by the oil pump upon initial starting of the engine. Additionally when very hot it must retain sufficient thickness to prevent metal-to-metal contact in the bearings.

Viscosity index   The viscosity index is a measure of change in viscosity of oil with a given change in temperature. Oils which suffer a large change like some of the older types have a low viscosity index and those with a comparatively small change have a high viscosity index. The term 'multi-grade' therefore implies an oil of high viscosity index and usually suitable for summer and winter use in temperate climates. Viscosity is measured by allowing a standard quantity of oil to flow through a standard measure under specified conditions. The time of flow is then taken as an indication of viscosity. The viscosity index is found by observing viscosity in this way at two specified temperatures and comparing the change with that produced in 'reference oils' at the same temperatures.

A good oil must have body as well as thickness. The difference between the two can be seen if you compare syrup with jam. As far as the flow rate through a standard measure is concerned, they would be about the same but the jam would come out in drops while the syrup would come out in a stream which would stretch a long way before it broke. The syrup can be said to have a much better body than the jam even though they have the same viscosity, but it's still no good for lubricating back axles! This body characteristic is vital in oil as layers must be maintained between rubbing surfaces. Therefore what is needed is an oil with a good body that will flow readily but will hold a strong film.

Classification of oils

The system of grading for crankcase oils in respect of viscosity in general use is that devised by the Society of Automotive Engineers (SAE). Although this is an American body the system is internationally known and recognised. The basis is the measurement of viscosity at one or other of two temperatures — $0^{\circ}F$ and $210^{\circ}F$. These are chosen as being reasonably typical of winter starting and summer running extremes of crankcase temperature. At $0^{\circ}F$ a range of viscosity suitable for typical engines is specified and subdivided into three sections classified as SAE5W, SAE10W and SAE20W. Similarly at $210^{\circ}F$ viscosity is chosen suitable for typical engines and now subdivided into four classifications, SAE20, SAE30, SAE40 and SAE50.

An older type 'summer' oil would fit one of the classifications at $210^{\circ}F$ but would be too thick for any of the classifications at $0^{\circ}F$. Conversely an old type winter oil would be too thin at $210^{\circ}F$.

Modern developments enable oils such as Castrol GTX to be produced that will meet both a summer and winter classification. It has a high viscosity index and as mentioned previously is known as 'multi-grade'.

Additives   The chemistry of the additives used in the production of lubricating oils is a very complex technology in its own right, successes in this field have made the modern high speed, high power units a practical proposition. It is sufficient for the present to consider three main functions in the general field of 'additives'.

1 Viscosity index improvers whose function is to give additional viscosity at high temperature without causing thickening at low temperatures.

2 Anti-wear additives To provide extra protection at very high temperatures and pressures, other special additives may be included. Castrol research has shown that under these conditions certain types of metallic compound would react to provide powerful localised protection precisely when and where needed.

3 Anti-oxidant additives Under the very high temperatures and pressures found in an engine, oil can be affected by oxygen and the by-products of combustion. When the petrol/air mixture burns, it produces water and acidic vapour. An untreated oil would be attacked and would deteriorate very quickly, becoming thick, discoloured and losing its lubricating qualities and body. This could result in a build-up of oxidised oil baked onto the pistons, trapping the piston rings in their grooves and preventing a gas-tight seal with the cylinder bore. To reduce the effects of oxidation to a minimum, special anti-oxidant additives are used. Those additives used in Castrol Oils are the most effective yet discovered.

Remember that the oil also has a vital job of cooling to do. It travels round the bearings and is sprayed into the pistons which are subjected to the full heat of combustion. Without the steady stream of oil to cool them, the pistons would burn and the bearings would overheat, causing excess friction which would quickly destroy them. This job as a coolant puts a heavy strain on the anti-oxidant additives in the oil.

with prolonged idling, regular short journey use or frequent cold weather starting.

When the time comes for the oil to be changed, obtain a fresh supply in sealed tins, a new filter, a tray to catch the old oil and a funnel.

Run the engine until it is hot to ensure that the oil collects sediment and will run out freely. Undo and remove the drain plug and let the oil run into the tray.

Two types of engine oil filter are fitted, the renewable element and the renewable canister type.

With the first type, remove the filter bowl, taking care to note the position of any springs and washers. Wash out the filter bowl and replace the rubber sealing ring in the filter housing. Prise out the old ring and carefully fit the new one supplied with the filter. Replace the filter and bowl with the springs and washers in their correct positions.

The second type is much easier to renew. Simply unscrew the old canister and discard. Smear a little engine oil onto the sealing ring and screw in the canister until it is hand tight.

Refit the drain plug and tighten securely. Refill the engine with the correct quantity of Castrol oil. Run the engine until the oil pressure warning light goes out (or the gauge registers a good reading), and then check the filter and

The engine oil change.

No matter how good the basic oil and its additives, it has a very definite life. After this, it is working below its best and the engine can be damaged as a result of wear. Therefore NEVER neglect oil change. Only by changing the oil at the manufacturer's recommended interval can the owner be sure of correct lubrication and protection from the by-products of combustion.

If the car is used mostly in traffic the oil is overworked, as it never really gets hot enough to boil off the water and contaminants it has removed from the engine and which it carries in solution to prevent their damaging the engine. To prolong the engine life the oil change period should be decreased as recommended by the manufacturer. This could mean changing oil every 3000 miles instead of every 6000 miles if the car is used mainly for stop-start motoring

The oil filter bowl type

sump plug for any signs of leaks.

The problem a lot of people have is disposing of the old oil. On no account should this be put down the public drainage system. Most council dustmen will take sealed metal cans with the refuse but the best method is to take it to a local garage who have special arrangements for disposal of waste oil.

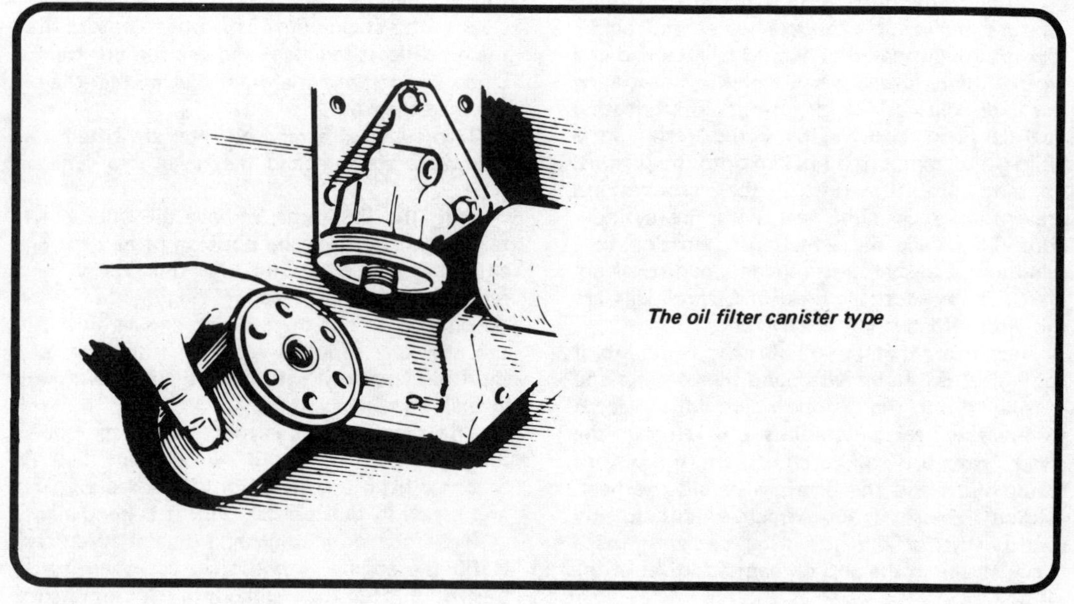

The oil filter canister type

The cooling system

Although the petrol engine is a heat producing engine in that the combustion of the mixture creates a great deal of heat, the engine must not be allowed to become too hot. It is the function of the cooling system to control this heat. The engine may be either water or air cooled.

Water cooled

The majority of car engines are liquid cooled with a coolant circulating around passages drilled (cast) into the cylinder head and block. Normally water is used, but in cold weather conditions the use of an antifreeze becomes necessary.

A typical sealed or closed cooling system is shown. This means that water continuously circulates around the system without the addition of fresh water with the exception of topping up to make up slight losses during servicing.

In earlier engines circulation was entirely due to thermo-syphon action. When water is heated it expands so that its density decreases and it tends to rise. The water in the passages and jacket surrounding the cylinders flows upwards and is replaced by cooler water entering the engine from the radiator.

The hot water passes from the top of the engine to the radiator where it is cooled by the passage of cold air through the core. However, a satisfactory thermo-syphon action is only obtained if there is a substantial head of water which means that the top of the radiator must be well above the top of the engine.

Water circulation in a thermo-syphon system is very sluggish and the modern engine is always fitted with a pump to provide a positive water flow. One advantage of this is that the water passages can be arranged to direct the flow onto such hot spots as around the exhaust valves and spark plugs.

The water pump is usually of the centrifugal impeller type and located in the water flow between the bottom of the radiator and the front of the engine. It is driven by the fan belt. The cooling water does not enter the engine at the bottom of the water jacket but at a point slightly higher up in the engine. This is to prevent undue disturbance of the water at a point in the engine which does not become excessively hot and which would otherwise tend to be over-cooled.

A thermostat is fitted into the cooling system to assist rapid warming up and control the coolant temperature. It is in the form of a valve placed in the outlet from the engine and operated by a liquid filled bellows or wax pellet element. When the engine is cold the valve is closed so restricting the water flow but as the engine warms up the element or wax pellet expands and opens the valve. In some systems the valve redirects the heated water through a pipe and back to the engine by-passing the radiator.

Nowadays the cooling system is pressurised so that the boiling point is raised. By sealing off the cooling system and fitting a pressure cap to the radiator it is possible to ensure that the water will not boil away even at high altitudes or with the engine working hard.

In modern cars the radiator is hidden behind a protective grille and sometimes ducting is fitted to direct air onto the radiator core.

To induce a reasonable flow of air through the radiator core when the car is moving slowly or stationary, a fan is normally fitted behind the radiator. It is driven directly from the engine by means of the vee belt which also drives the generator.

Air cooling

Air cooled engines have always been in the minority because it is difficult to air cool multi-cylinder engines evenly. Also air cooled engines tend to be more noisy than water cooled because water absorbs a considerable amount of general engine noise. The cylinders are finned to increase the heat dissipation area and because there is insufficient natural draught in a closed engine compartment it is necessary to fit a cowling around the engine. An engine driven blower fan is used to direct a vast volume of air around the cowling.

The main advantages of air cooling are that no problems arise with the coolant freezing or boiling and engine construction can be simpler.

Antifreeze

This mixes with the water to give a solution with a very low freezing point. A range of concentrations are recommended for protection down to various temperatures and the cars handbook will tell you the correct amount for the system, or the local garage will have a chart. There is a large variety of chemicals which will lower the freezing point of water. Many have serious drawbacks in that they will corrode the inside of the engine and radiator or boil out of the water at a low temperature. Castrol Antifreeze is a carefully selected blend of chemicals which will not cause corrosion, even to aluminium engines, will maintain a high boiling point used and in the recommended quantity, will give full protection against freezing.

Before adding antifreeze, run the engine and check for any signs of leaks. Tighten all the hose clips just to be sure, drain the radiator and flush through thoroughly with clean water. Pour in the antifreeze and after topping up with water, run the engine at fast tickover for a few minutes to make sure that the antifreeze is fully mixed and circulated. Most radiators need periodic topping up but in winter remember that adding straight water is diluting the antifreeze solution, so when it is necessary to top up, use the recommended proportion of antifreeze with the water.

Water-cooled engines *keep an even temperature by circulating a steady flow of water through special passages in the engine and to the radiator. The flow is maintained by the water pump. To give a quick warm up period when the engine is started from cold, a thermostat prevents water from flowing through the radiator until the engine has reached working temperature. A fan is included to keep the engine cool in traffic, and the most common cause of over-heating is a loose fan belt.*

Air-cooled engines *use a very large fan to keep a steady flow of air over the cylinder housings. This fan is normally belt driven and care must be taken to see that the belt is tight and in good condition. Once the fan ceases to work, dangerous temperatures are reached very quickly.*

Cooling system - maintenance

Regularly check all hoses for signs of perishing and the hose clips for security. If in doubt it is better to err on the right side and fit a new hose.

To ensure that the water pump operates correctly check the fan belt tension and adjust to the manufacturers recommended tension.

Before the winter starts check that the anti-freeze in the cooling system is up to strength at a local garage or fill the cooling system with fresh.

Some water pumps have a grease nipple or plug that must be removed and grease inserted at recommended intervals.

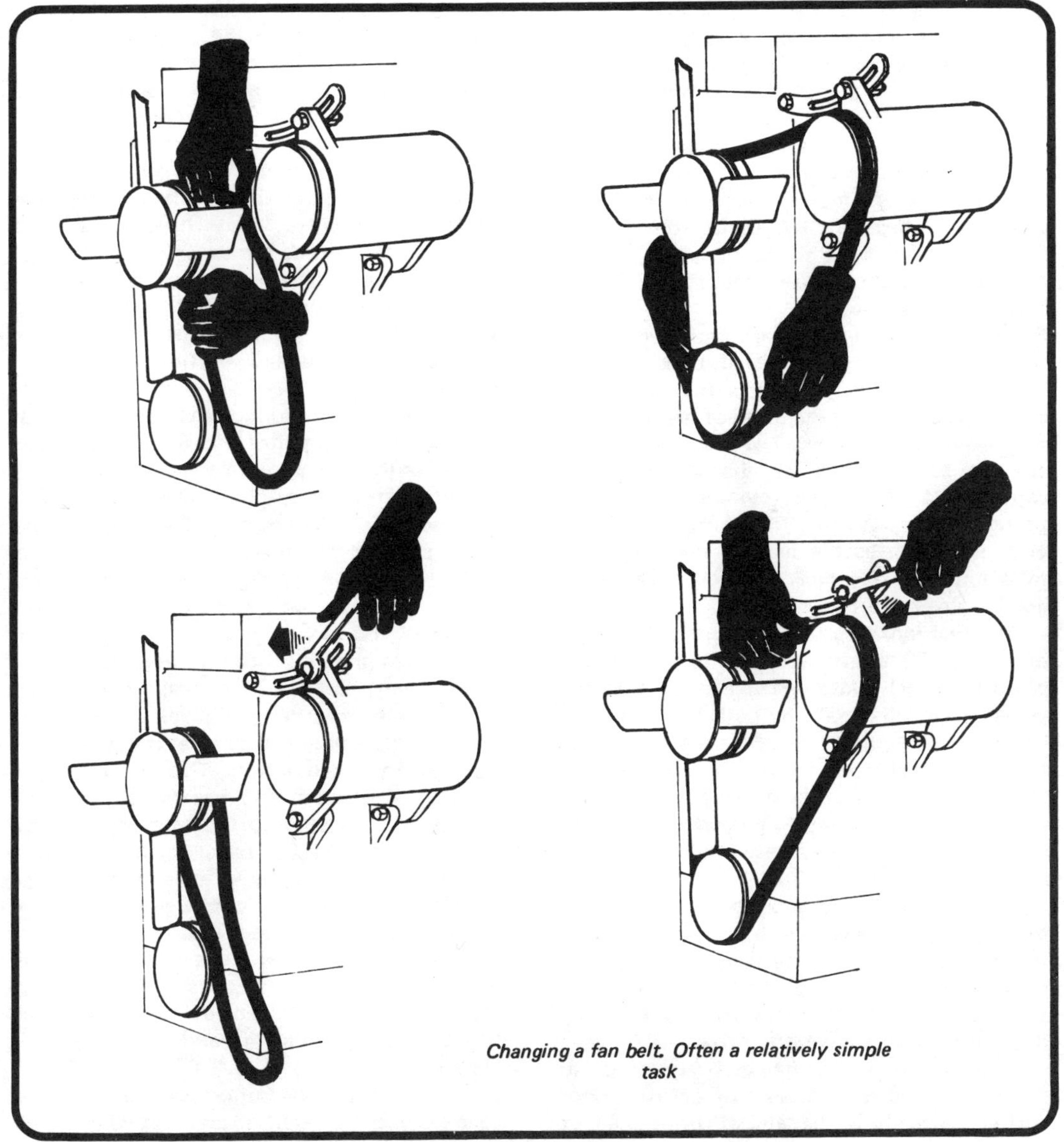

Changing a fan belt. Often a relatively simple task

The fuel system

Most motor car engines use petrol as a fuel. The fuel system of every engine comprises the tank for storing the fuel, the fuel pump for pumping the fuel to the carburettor and the carburettor for mixing the correct proportion of petrol and air together. Various connecting pipe lines and filters are also fitted.

The complete fuel system may be divided into two separate sections:

1 The fuel delivery section which is concerned with raising the liquid from the fuel tank and delivering it to the float bowl of the carburettor in a quantity proportional to the engine requirements.

2 The second is the vapourising section in which the fuel is drawn off through a jet or series of jets in the form of a fine spray and carried into the inlet manifold of the engine by the ingoing stream of air. The mixture of petrol and air so produced by the carburettor is carried into the engine cylinders. The proportion of air and fuel mixed by the carburettor is known as the air/fuel ratio and this ratio must be accurately controlled to ensure good engine performance.

The fuel tank is usually mounted at the rear of the car for safety reasons. From here it is piped to a fuel pump which may be operated either electrically from the battery or mechanically from the engine camshaft. Its function is to pump petrol from the tank and deliver it to the carburettor. A fine mesh filter is often fitted into a fuel pump to exclude particles of dirt or dust which may have found their way into the tank.

The carburettor is mounted on the inlet manifold which leads to each inlet valve port on the side of the cylinder head. It is through the passages of the inlet manifold that the engine piston draws in the fuel mixture, past the open inlet valve, on its Induction Stroke.

The function of the carburettor is to produce the correct mixture of petrol vapour and air, normally in the ratio of about one part by weight of petrol to fifteen of air.

The air passage in the carburettor is at one point slightly reduced in diameter and this has the effect of increasing the air velocity passing through it. At this same point is a fuel spraying orifice which is fed by a constant level fuel chamber. This level is kept at a constant by a float and valve. When fuel is used, the level will drop and with it the float, so opening the valve which allows the fuel level to be restored. This chamber is called a 'float chamber' and it is vented to the outside atmosphere.

When the engine is running, air is drawn through the carburettor and at the point where the restriction is formed in the carburettor air passage the accelerated air flow will create a partial vacuum.

The fuel level in the float chamber is so arranged that the petrol rises in the spraying jet almost to its discharge point.

With normal atmospheric pressure acting on the surface of the petrol in the float chamber and a reduced pressure in the restricted part of the carburettor air passage, fuel will flow out of the jet and into the air stream. It is instantly vaporised and carried into the engine cylinders in the form of a highly combustible mixture.

Located between the fuel spraying jet and the inlet manifold is a pivoting disc which controls the amount of air that is able to flow through the carburettor. This is called the 'throttle valve' and the spindle on which it rotates is connected to the accelerator pedal. When the accelerator pedal is depressed the throttle valve is rotated so allowing the engine to draw in more fresh petrol/air mixture and increase its running speed. When the accelerator pedal is gradually released the throttle valve will move back to the closed position and restrict the amount of fresh petrol/air mixture which the engine can draw in and so its speed is reduced.

On many types of carburettor a second valve called the 'choke' is fitted and located in the air

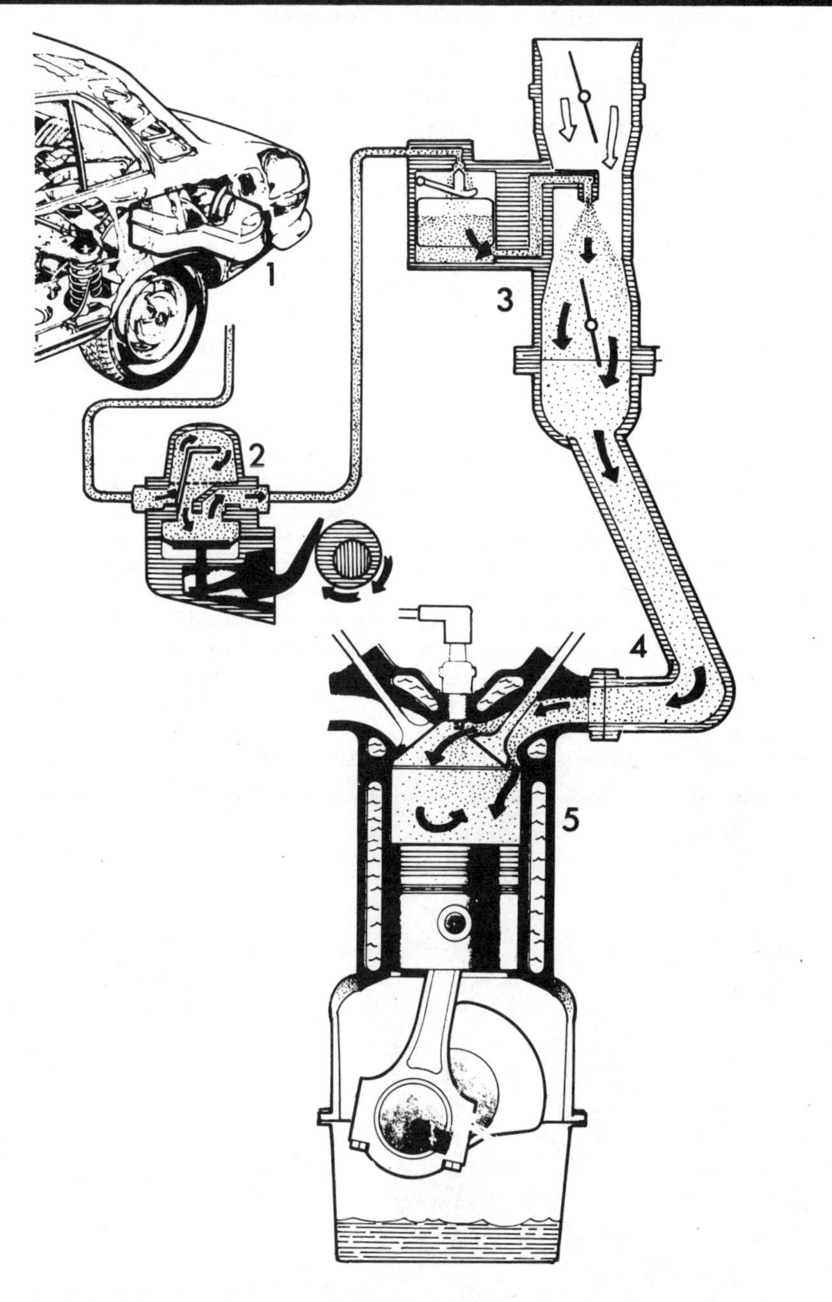

The fuel system "flow line"

1 Fuel tank   2 Fuel pump   3 Carburettor 4 Inlet manifold   5 Cylinder

intake side of the carburettor body. It restricts the amount of fresh air which is allowed to enter the carburettor and so enables a richer than normal petrol/air mixture to be drawn into the engine to help start the engine when it is cold.

The modern carburettor is a very complicated instrument and is fitted with many other devices to allow for variations in petrol/air ratio to be obtained for conditions such as engine idling, sudden acceleration and high speed motions.

Carburettors are often classified according to the direction in which the fresh air flows through the carburettor body. Those in which the flow is directly upwards are termed vertical or updraught carburettors. Most common is the downdraught type in which the air passes vertically downwards.

The sidedraught carburettor is also commonly used. In this case the fresh air enters directly sideways which means that it can be mounted so as to feed straight into the inlet manifold thereby reducing the number of bends which the petrol/air mixture has to negotiate.

A compromise between downdraught and sidedraught carburettors is sometimes used, this being known as the semi-downdraught carburettor.

An air cleaner is fitted onto the air intake of most carburettors to remove particles of dust and so helps to reduce engine wear. A second function of the air cleaner is that it serves to silence the rush of air into the carburettor air intake.

Fuel system - maintenance

A carburettor is a precision instrument, it must be treated as such. If it must be taken apart wash it carefully in petrol and blow out the jets. Do NOT poke them with wire as this can enlarge the holes and increase fuel consumption.

Always renew the air cleaner element at the periods recommended by the manufacturer. Failure to do so will affect engine performance and increase fuel consumption.

Regularly clean the fuel filters. One is usually located in the fuel pump and an additional canister type filter is sometimes fitted in the main fuel line to the fuel pump.

To ensure ease of operation lubricate all controls and external moving parts with a little engine oil.

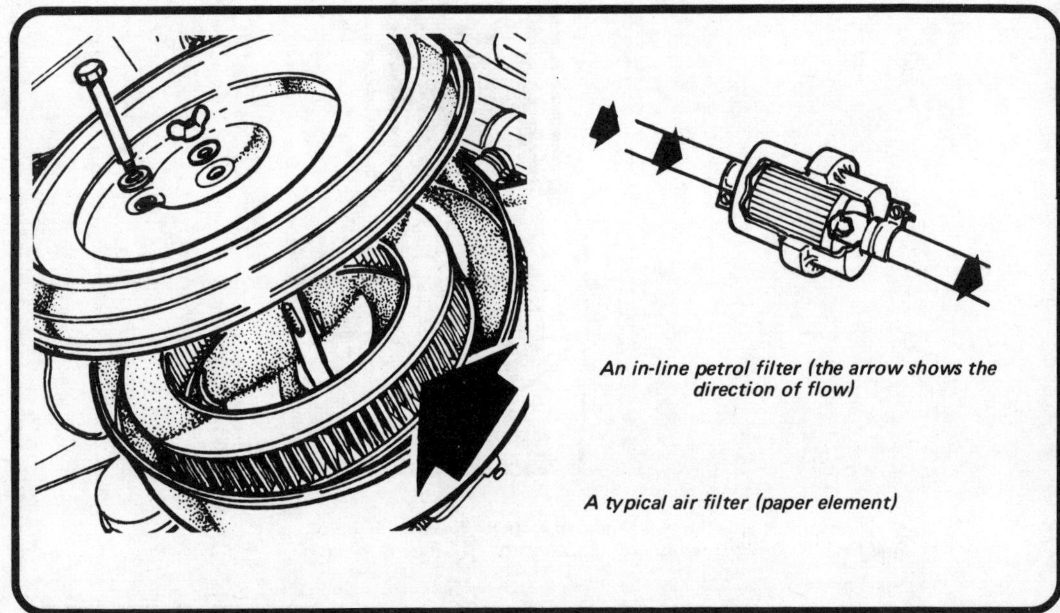

An in-line petrol filter (the arrow shows the direction of flow)

A typical air filter (paper element)

The ignition system

The function of the ignition system is to provide a spark in the combustion chamber to ignite the mixture at the correct time. The system comprises the battery, coil, distributor and spark plugs.

Ignition coil

The ignition coil produces the high voltage that is required to make the spark at the spark plugs. It comprises two coils of insulated wire which are wound one on top of the other in such a manner that the number of turns in the inner coil (secondary windings) are very much greater than that in the outer coil (primary windings).

If a low voltage is supplied to the primary coil and suddenly switched off a momentary impulse at a very much higher voltage is induced in the secondary coil. Battery voltage is supplied to the primary coil (low tension) resulting in voltages in the region of 10,000 - 15,000 volts being created in the secondary (high tension).

The switching arrangement is performed by the contact breaker points in the distributor.

Distributor

The distributor has two functions to perform:

1 To make and break the low tension (LT) supply to the ignition coil.
2 To distribute the high tension (HT) supply created by the ignition coil to each spark plug at the correct moment.

The distributor comprises a casing which contains a central spindle which is normally driven by the engine camshaft. The top end of the shaft has a four lobe cam (four cylinder engine) or six lobe cam (six cylinder engine) mounted on it which opens the contact breaker points as it rotates. The contact breaker points close again under the action of a spring which rests on the arm holding one of the contact points (moving point).

A rotor arm is mounted on the top of the shaft and it has a metal contact which will pass by the segments in the distributor cap.

Most distributors have an internal arrangement whereby the ignition timing can be automatically advanced or retarded to suit the engine speed and load. This is carried out by centrifugal weights and by a vacuum unit which is connected to the carburettor.

The distributor cap comprises an insulated casing which contains a centre contact normally in the form of a spring loaded carbon brush. This is connected to the high tension supply from the ignition coil.

The distributor cap also contains one metal segment (contact) for each spark plug which is connected to the spark plug by a high tension lead.

The centre HT contact rests on the centre of the metal contact of the rotor arm and as the rotor arm rotates the end of the metal contact lines up with each spark plug segment in the distributor cap. The HT supply therefore passes through the distributor cap and passes to each spark plug in turn in a pre-determined order known as the firing order.

Spark plug

One spark plug is fitted to each cylinder and is simply a carrier of electrodes between which the spark is created. It comprises a metal body which is screwed into the cylinder head at the top of the combustion chamber.

An insulator in the spark plug body contains a central electrode onto which the high tension spark plug lead is attached. A second or side electrode is attached to the bottom of the spark plug body so that it reaches out and over the end of the centre electrode. A small gap between the two electrodes is adjustable to compensate for erosion.

Whenever a high tension impulse is passed through the distributor cap to the spark plug it passes down the centre electrode and jumps the

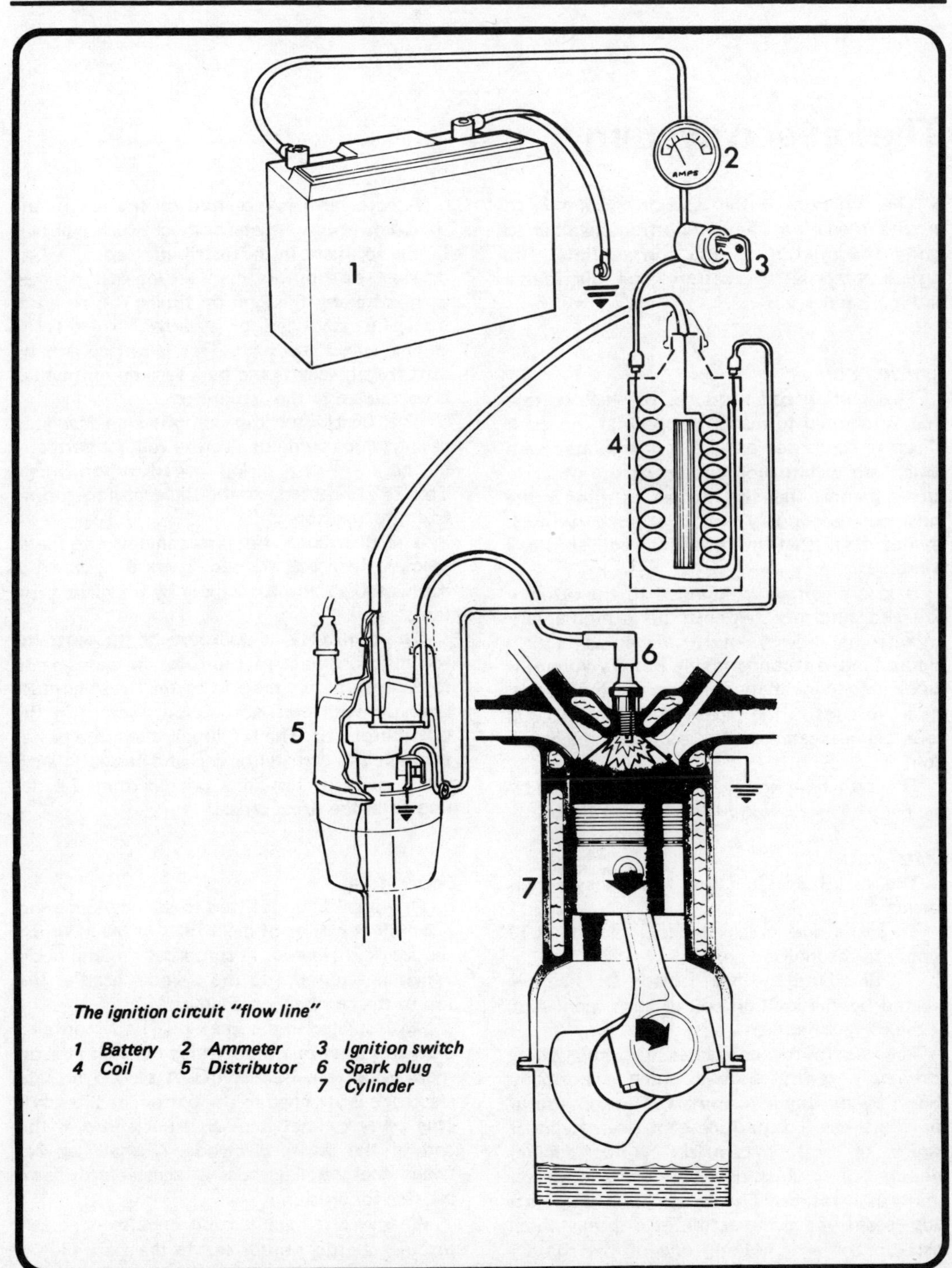

The ignition circuit "flow line"

1 Battery   2 Ammeter   3 Ignition switch
4 Coil   5 Distributor   6 Spark plug
                    7 Cylinder

gap to the side electrode in the form of a large blue spark.

Ignition system - maintenance

Inspect the spark plug leads from time to time to ensure that they are not damaged as this can lead to non-starting and incorrect running, especially under damp conditions.

The spark plugs should be periodically cleaned and tested at a local garage. When it becomes necessary to renew the plugs ensure that the recommended type is used as spark plugs are available in a wide range of types and sizes.

Check the tightness of the spark plugs from time to time but do not overtighten. A loose spark plug can overheat because the plug depends on good contact at its seating washer to conduct away the heat. If the washers have flattened they should be renewed.

Generally speaking it is a good practice to fit a new set of spark plugs every 10,000 miles.

The appearance of the interior of the spark plug is a good indication as to the running conditions of the engine and can reveal faults in the ignition system, lubrication system, carburation on the plug itself.

When the spark plugs are being checked the contact breaker points should also be checked for pitting or incorrect gap. Clean and reset as necessary.

Systematically check the cleanliness and security of all LT and HT leads connected with the ignition system.

Remove the distributor cap and lubricate the contact breaker moving point pivot and the automatic advance/retard system with a little engine oil. Smear a little grease on the cam face. Refit the distributor cap.

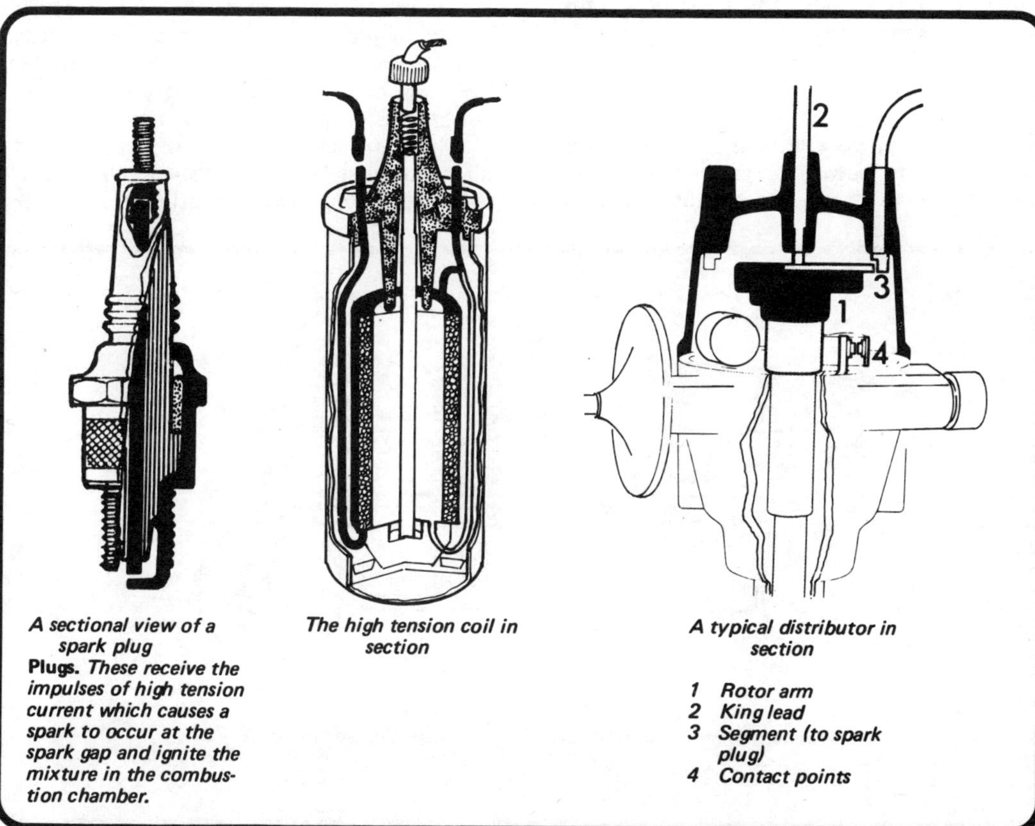

A sectional view of a spark plug
Plugs. *These receive the impulses of high tension current which causes a spark to occur at the spark gap and ignite the mixture in the combustion chamber.*

The high tension coil in section

A typical distributor in section

1   *Rotor arm*
2   *King lead*
3   *Segment (to spark plug)*
4   *Contact points*

The transmission

The transmission system transfers the power created in the engine to the road wheels. It may be considered in three parts.

1 the clutch,
2 the gearbox,
3 the final drive,

regardless of the layout of the car, whether it be a front wheel drive car with its engine, gearbox and final drive as one complete unit or a conventional car with the engine at the front driving the rear wheels. The function of the units remains the same.

The clutch

On all cars fitted with manual transmission (as opposed to automatic transmission), the clutch comprises three parts, a thrust bearing, a pressure plate and a driven plate. The action is very simple. The driven plate is a metal disc which is covered on both sides with a high friction material, and its centre is splined so that it is positively located on the gearbox input shaft. It is positioned between the engine flywheel and pressure plate which is so called because it is fitted with heavy springs which force the driven plate onto the flywheel. The friction material ensures that the driven plate and the flywheel move at the same speed, so that as long as the driven plate is sandwiched between the pressure plate and the flywheel by the force of the springs in the pressure plate, power is transmitted to the gearbox.

When the clutch pedal is depressed the thrust bearing is pushed against the pressure plate. This compresses the springs so taking the

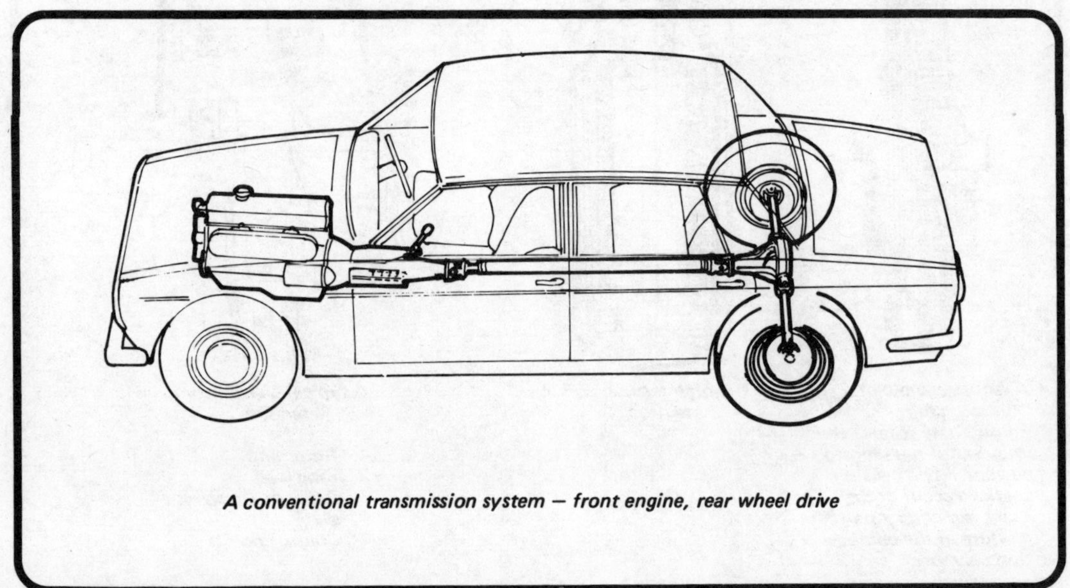

A conventional transmission system — front engine, rear wheel drive

tension off the driven plate and prevents power from being transmitted from the engine to the gearbox.

Upon releasing the clutch pedal the springs force the driven plate against the flywheel and allow drive to be transmitted from the engine to the gearbox.

Over a period of time, the friction material on the driven plate, which is similar to that as used in brake linings, wears away.

Modern clutches are usually self adjusting to compensate for this wear.

 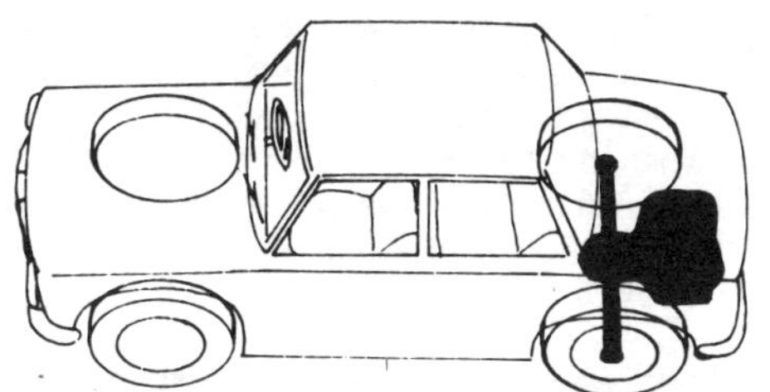

Two alternatives — left; front engine, front wheel drive, and right; rear engine, rear wheel drive

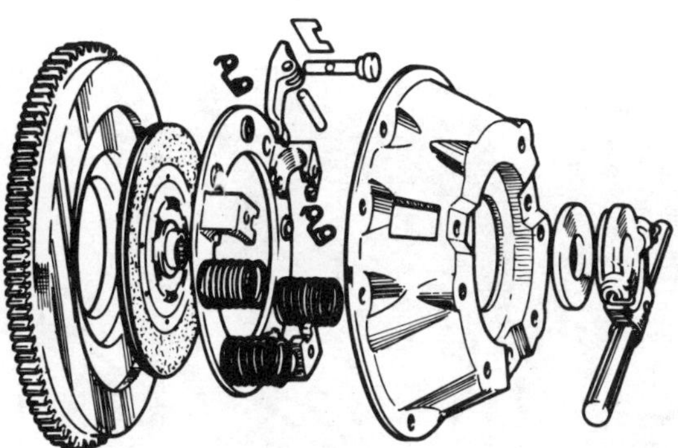

Spring clutch assembly. The springs force the pressure plate to sandwich the driven plate onto the flywheel face. The friction materials on the face of the driven plate ensures that full power is transmitted to the gearbox. Pressing the clutch pedal compresses the springs, freeing the driven plate and disconnecting the drive to the gearbox.

Diaphragm clutch assembly. In principle, this works exactly the same way as the spring clutch. The advantage of the diaphragm is that it holds its tension longer than springs. When the clutch pedal is depressed the centre of the diaphragm travels forwards releasing the pressure on the driven plate by an 'over-centre' action

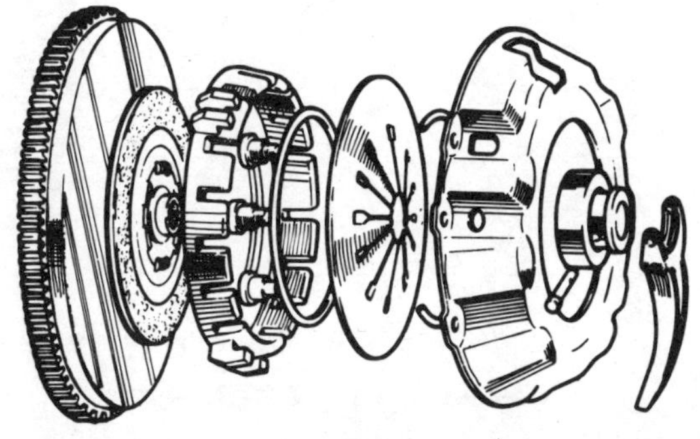

The gearbox

The function of the gearbox is to multiply engine torque. Torque is the turning force produced by the engine when combustion of the petrol/air mixture occurs. This is passed from the engine where it is produced to the driving wheels by the transmission, and the amount transmitted is controlled by the accelerator pedal and the selection of gears.

The lower the gear, the higher the multiplication factor. Its action is similar to that of a lever, when the longer the lever (away from its fulcrum point) is used the easier it is to move a weight - but also the longer the lever the further the end has to travel.

Similarly, low gears give the torque required to move the car from rest, but the engine speed increases very rapidly. Once the car is moving and has momentum, less torque is needed at the driving wheels so a higher gear and lower engine speed can be selected.

The action of the gearbox is shown in the figure on page 33. Changing gear is made smoother by the action of synchromesh, which is a friction joint that opposes the final engagement of the gears as they slide along their shafts. It does this to make both gear wheels move at the same speed. Trying to mesh two gears rotating at different speeds is the cause of noisy gear changing.

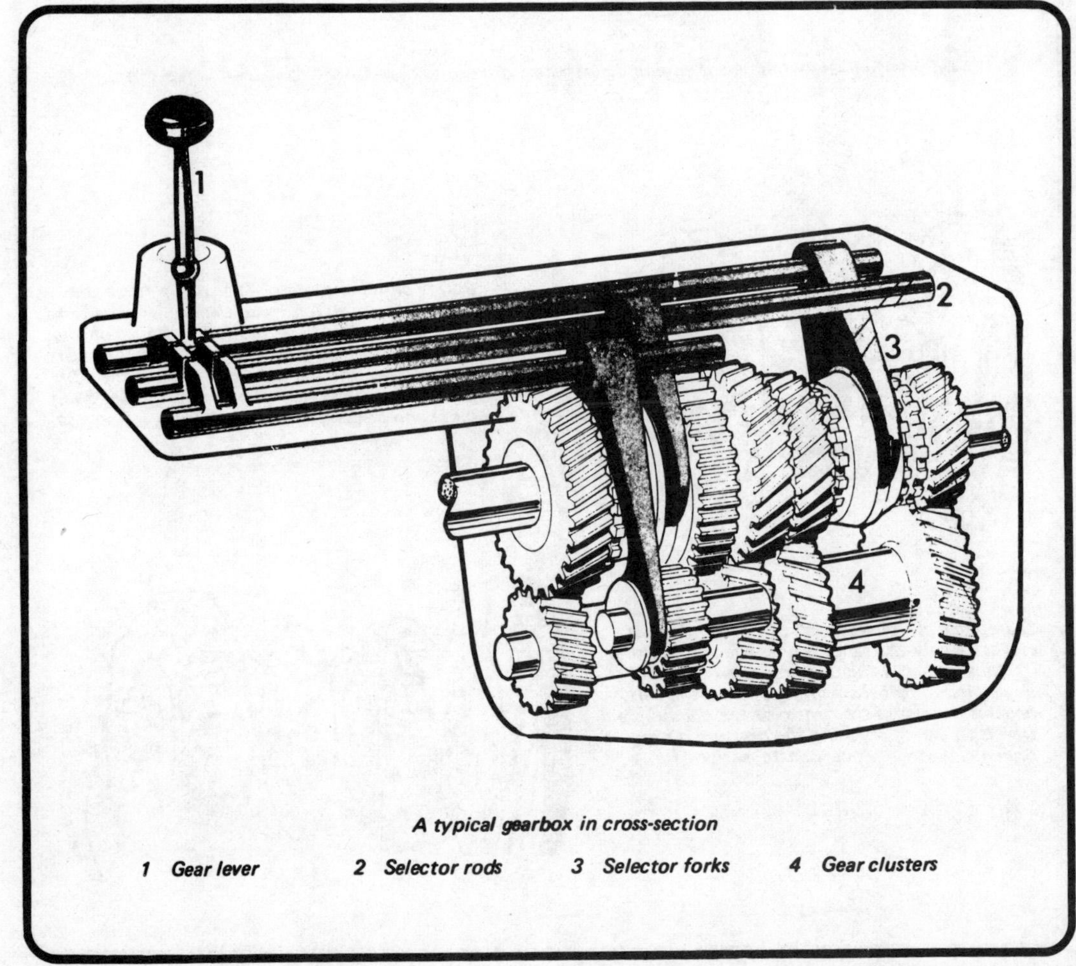

A typical gearbox in cross-section

1 Gear lever   *2 Selector rods*   *3 Selector forks*   *4 Gear clusters*

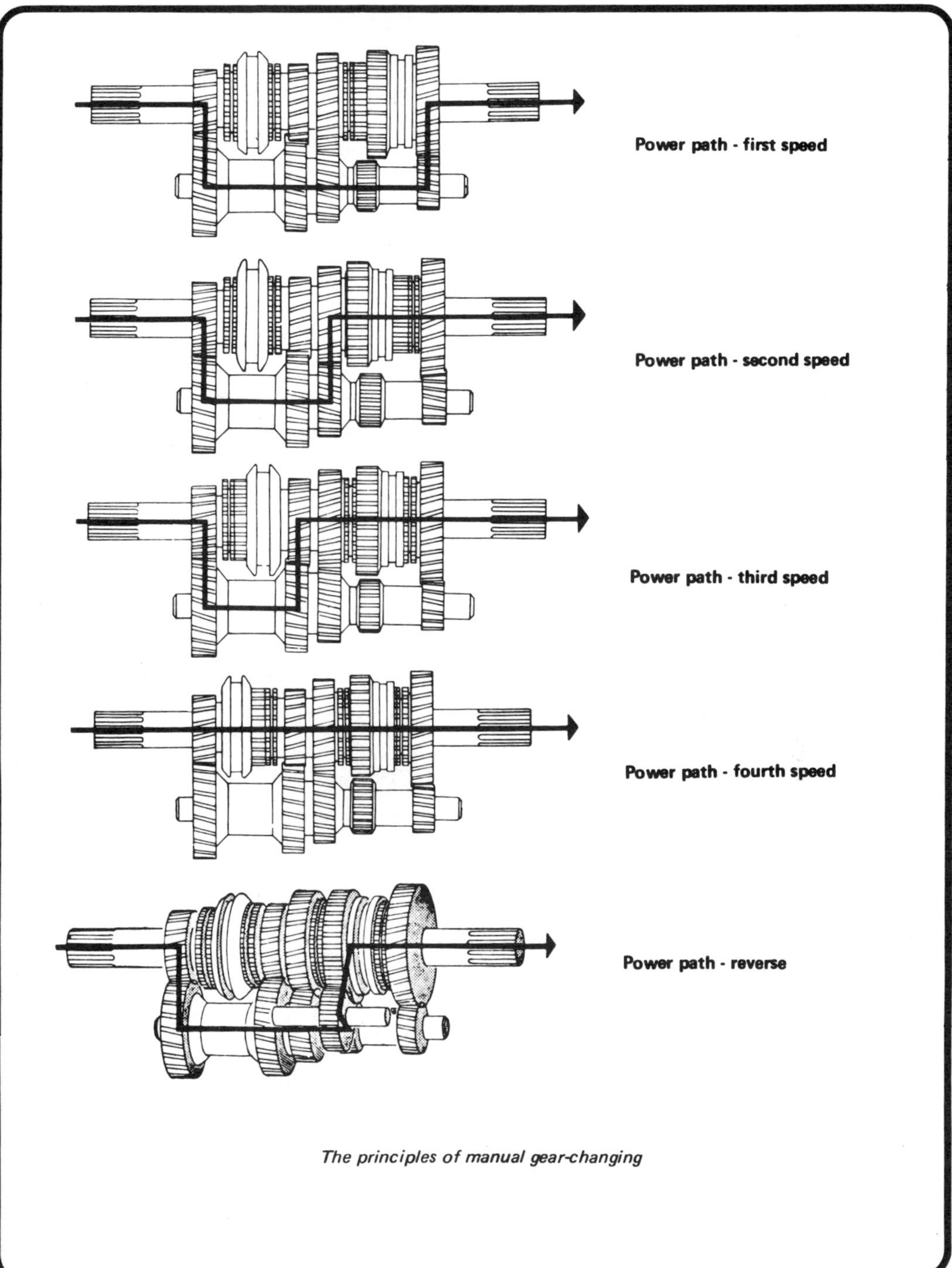

The principles of manual gear-changing

The final drive

This comprises the final drive gear and differential unit. The final drive gear ratio is selected such that the top gear of the gearbox can be a straight or direct connection between the engine and final drive. This is done to minimise power loss.

The differential allows the two driven wheels to move at different speeds when turning corners. If a fixed axle were used it would mean that the inner wheel would have to slip - with drastic results to the tyre treads and road holding.

With a differential the axle shaft is divided into separate shafts, one for each wheel, and appropriately called a halfshaft.

The inner end of each halfshaft is fitted with a bevel pinion, and these engage with two free pinions carried in a casing on the crownwheel. When the car is being driven in a straight line, the four pinions of the differential remain fixed in their relationship, but when the car begins to go round a corner the differential provides a variable ratio of speeds between the two halfshafts. The power is, in fact, being transmitted at different speeds via the free pinion on the crownwheel.

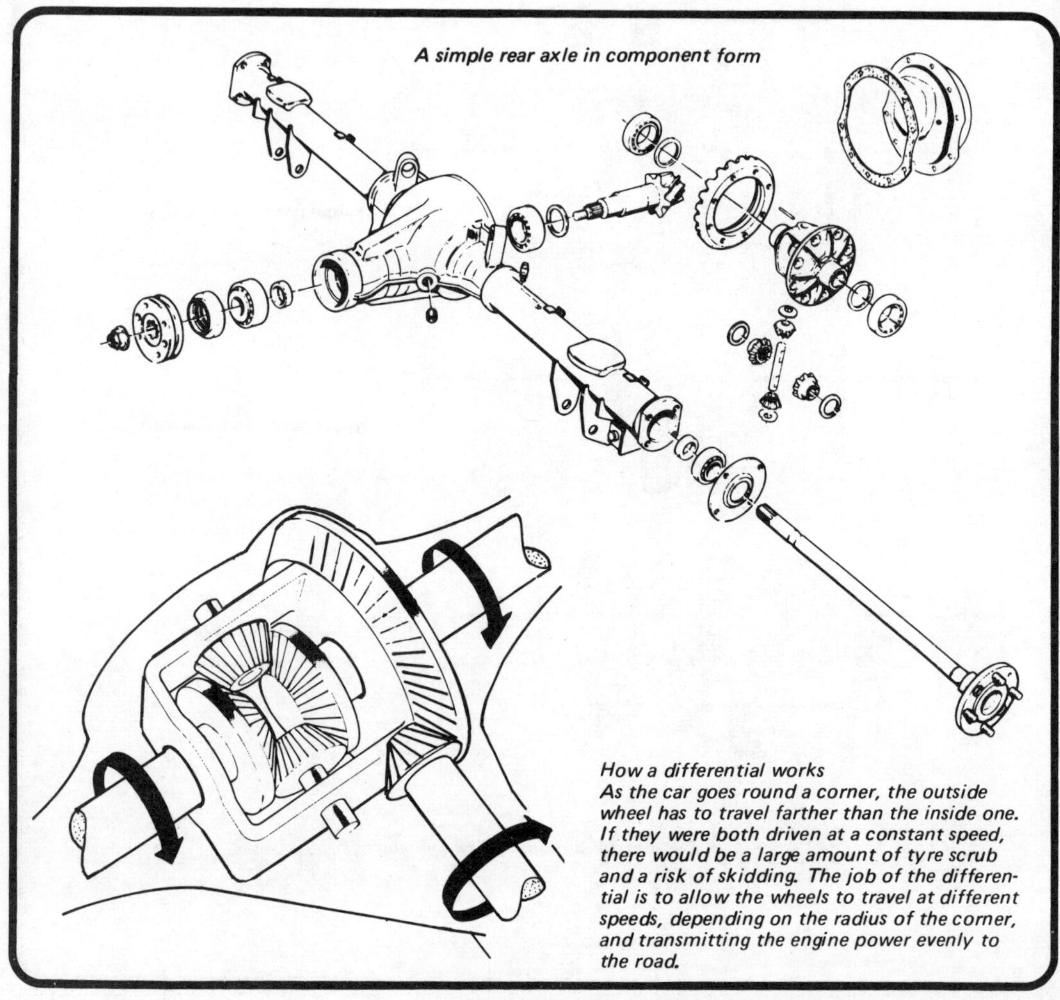

How a differential works
As the car goes round a corner, the outside wheel has to travel farther than the inside one. If they were both driven at a constant speed, there would be a large amount of tyre scrub and a risk of skidding. The job of the differential is to allow the wheels to travel at different speeds, depending on the radius of the corner, and transmitting the engine power evenly to the road.

Automatic transmission

Semi and fully automatic transmissions are becoming more popular as an alternative to a manual gearbox.

A semi-automatic system includes a clutch and gearbox and the driver is still able to select the required gear but without having to depress a clutch pedal. It amounts to being an automatic clutch.

With a fully automatic system the driver does not have to operate a clutch pedal or gear lever, When the accelerator pedal is depressed the car begins to move and thereafter all gears are changed up or down automatically depending on the engine load, road speed and position of the accelerator pedal.

On many fully automatic systems it is possible to override the automatic changing system so providing a hold or lock in a particular gear. This is particularly useful when towing caravans travelling in hilly districts.

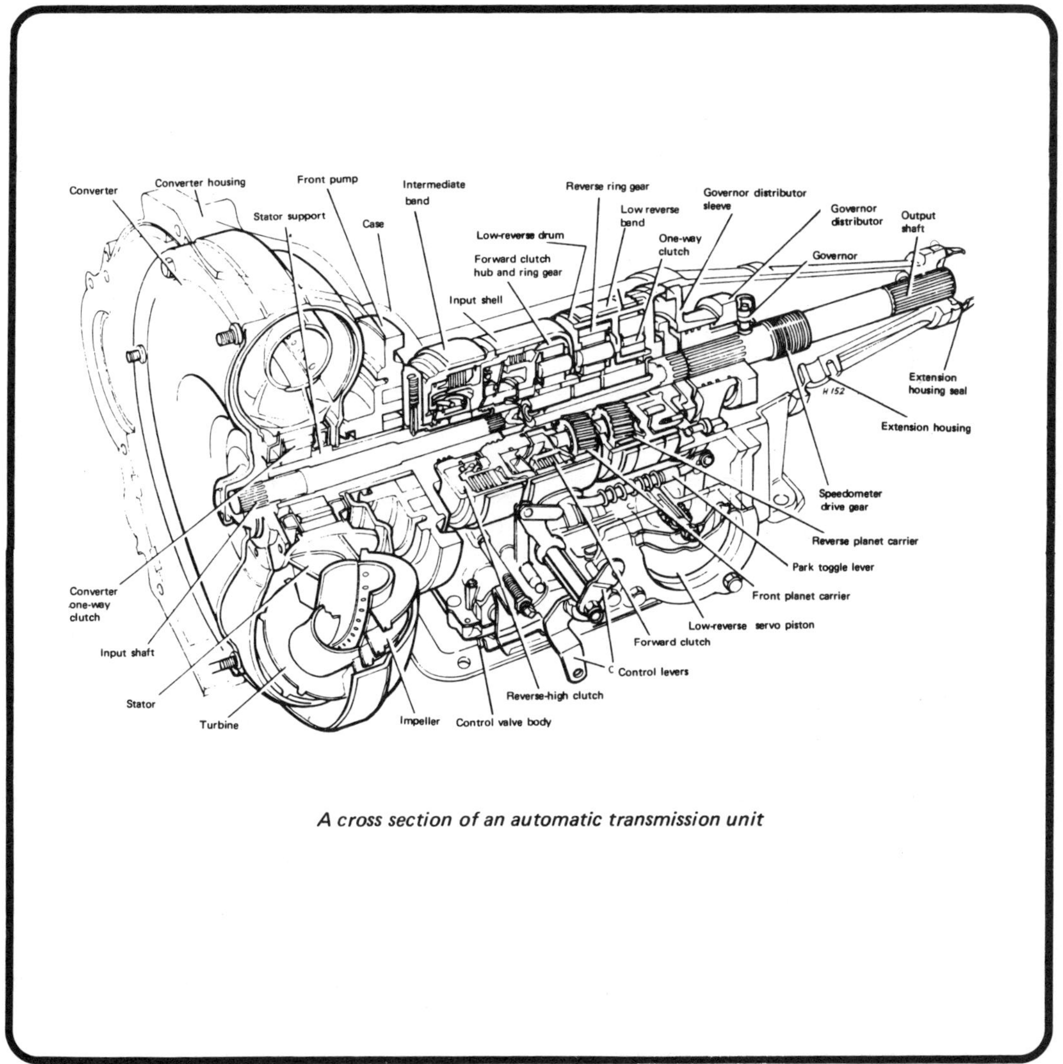

A cross section of an automatic transmission unit

Transmission system - lubrication maintenance

Many other parts beside the engine need lubrication. For the gearbox, oil is poured in through a hole in the casing. This hole has a cap or plug which screws into place. To reach it on some modern cars a rubber plug must be removed from the floor pressing. Its exact location is usually given in the car handbook but is commonly part way down on the side of the box, and its height above the bottom of the box decides the amount of oil that can be poured in. Do not attempt to overfill the gearbox or serious oil leaks can occur.

When an automatic transmission unit is fitted rigidly follow the manufacturers instructions for checking the oil level and topping up.

The back axle also requires lubrication and the filler plug is low enough in the casing to prevent overfilling.

Always use the correct amount of the recommended grade of oil because the action of gear teeth imposes severe loads on the lubricating oils. The action of the gearbox and final drive is to multiply engine torque and it can do so by as much as twenty times.

When a British Leyland front wheel drive car is owned it should be remembered that the engine, gearbox and differential/final drive share a common lubrication system. Regular oil changing is essential.

If a steering column change or remote control system is fitted do not forget to regularly lubricate the linkage.

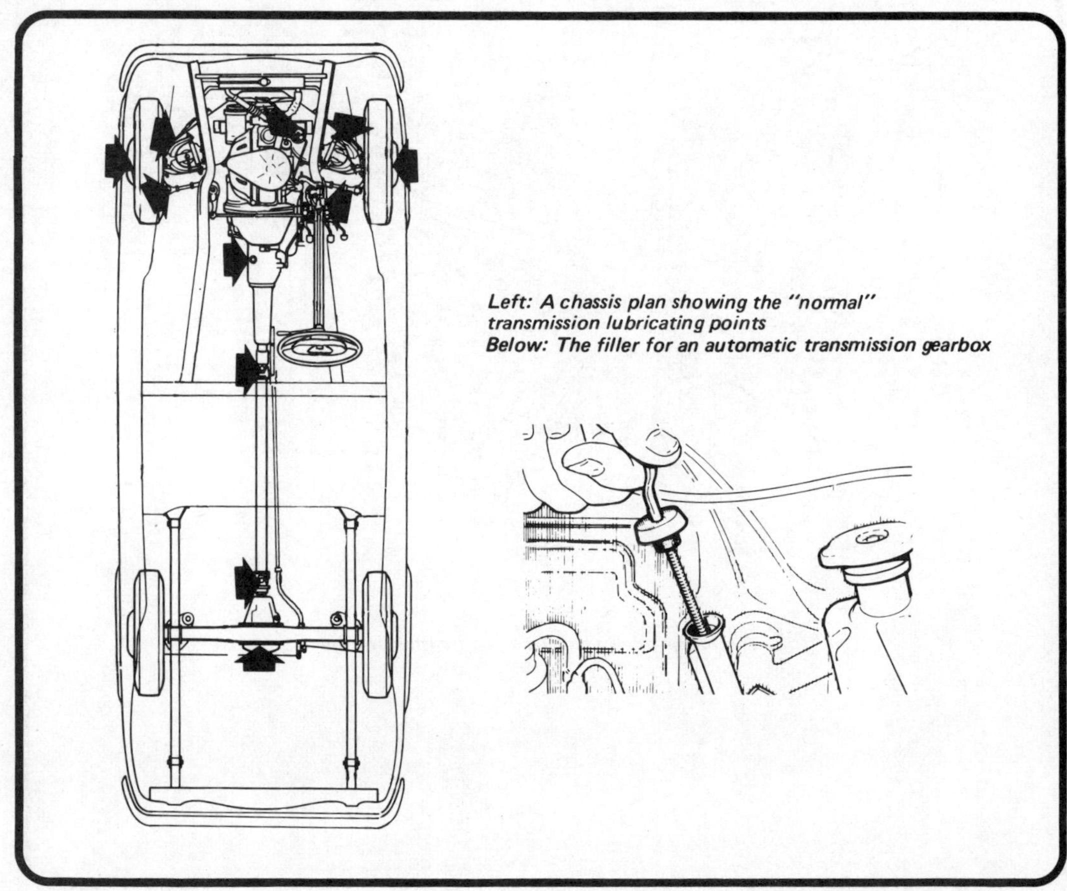

Left: A chassis plan showing the "normal" transmission lubricating points
Below: The filler for an automatic transmission gearbox

The brakes

The braking system is one part of the car that certainly does not want to be without friction. It is put to very good use to stop the car, because the action of the braking system is to transform the rolling energy of the car into heat energy at the brakes and to then lose that heat to the air. In the case of disc brakes some of the heat is dissipated through the metal components to the fluid line.

There are two basic types of brakes - disc and drum. They both use hydraulic pressure to force a high friction material against a moving surface, heat is generated as a result. In the case of the drum brake the linings are inside the drum and are forced outwards against the drum. With the disc brake, the disc rotates between the brake pads which are forced inwards onto the disc when hydraulic pressure is applied. The heat must be dissipated for the brakes to remain efficient.

Drum brakes

Each drum brake assembly comprises a pair of semi-circular brake shoes which are mounted on a fixed backplate and located inside a drum which rotates with the road wheel.

One end of each brake shoe is pivoted on a spindle or steady post and the other end held by a spring in contact with the piston of a hydraulic cylinder. In front brake assemblies it is usual to use two hydraulic cylinders so that the pressures exerted by the shoes are equalised.

Each brake shoe is faced with a brake lining which is a high frictional resistance material.

The hydraulic system consists of a master cylinder and slave cylinders (wheel cylinders) and interconnected with metal pipes and flexible hoses.

A piston in the master cylinder is connected to the brake pedal so that when the brake pedal is depressed the hydraulic fluid is forced out to each slave cylinder where it operates the pistons and forces the shoes against the brake drums. As the pedal is released a spring in the master cylinder and strong springs on the brake shoe webs return the shoes, the pistons and the fluid to their original positions.

The brakes can be operated by either a mechanical linkage from the brake pedal and handbrake lever but it is now more usual to operate the brakes from the brake pedal hydraulically and the handbrake lever alone mechanically.

One main advantage of hydraulic operation is that the system is self balancing which means that the same degree of pressure is automatically produced at each brake whereas mechanical linkages have to be very carefully adjusted for balance.

The handbrake mechanical linkage operates on the rear brakes only through a system of rods and/or cables connecting the handbrake lever to the brake shoe mechanisms. These operate independently of the hydraulic system.

Disc brakes

The disc brake comprises a steel disc with friction pads which are operated by hydraulic slave cylinders. The steel disc rotates with the wheel and at one point it is partially surrounded by a caliper which contains the two friction pads, one either side, and two hydraulic cylinders.

When the brake pedal is depressed the hydraulic pistons force the pads against the sides of the disc so creating a clamping action.

Because the disc is not enclosed, the heat generated when the brakes are applied is dissipated very much more quickly than it is from drum brakes, and this makes the disc brake less prone to fade.

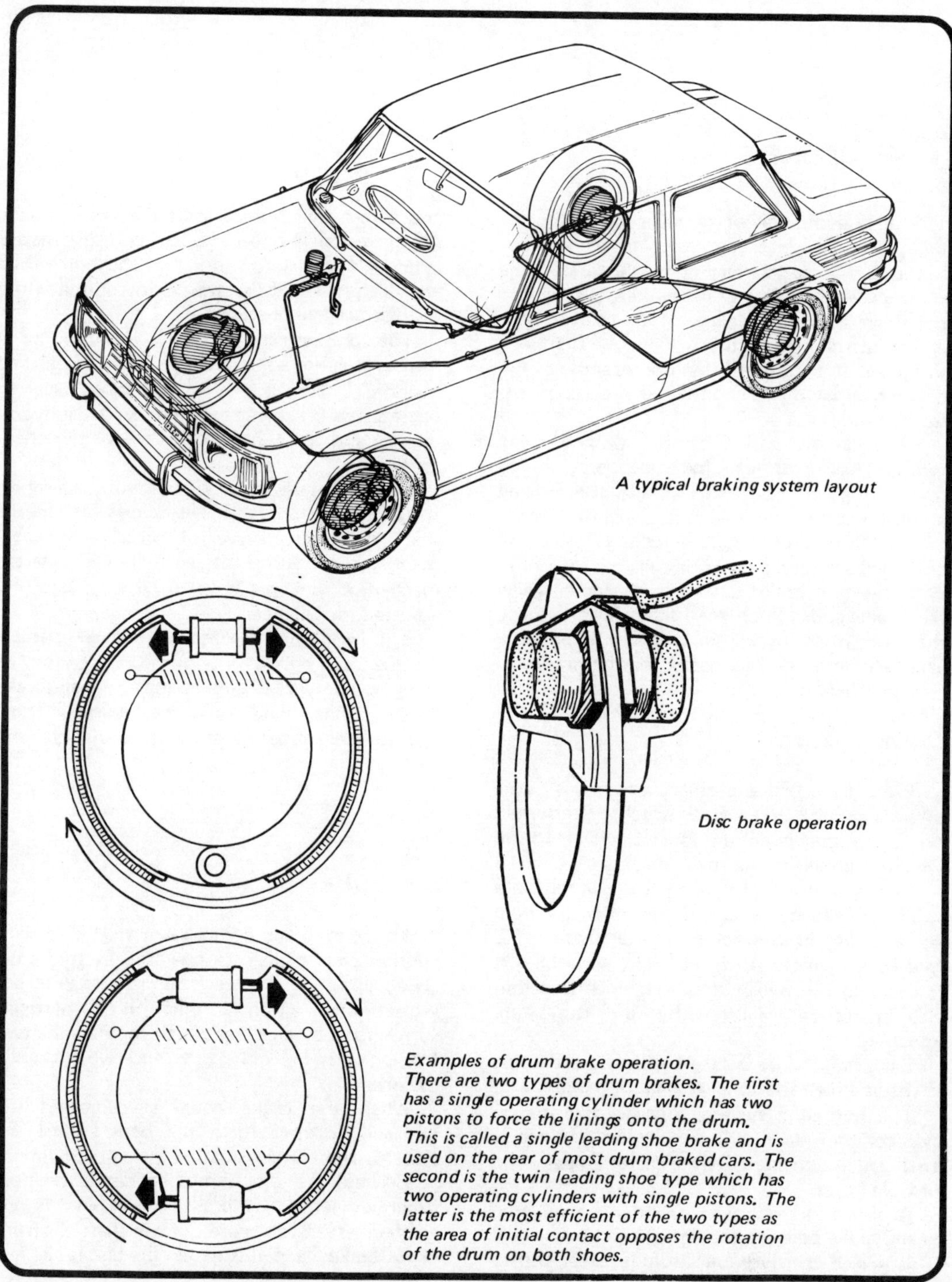

A typical braking system layout

Disc brake operation

*Examples of drum brake operation.
There are two types of drum brakes. The first
has a single operating cylinder which has two
pistons to force the linings onto the drum.
This is called a single leading shoe brake and is
used on the rear of most drum braked cars. The
second is the twin leading shoe type which has
two operating cylinders with single pistons. The
latter is the most efficient of the two types as
the area of initial contact opposes the rotation
of the drum on both shoes.*

Servo unit

Power assisted brakes are fitted to many modern cars or at least are available as an optional extra. They help to equate the limited strength of the driver with the large braking faces sometimes required, especially in the case of motor cars fitted with disc brakes.

The systems generally use the engine inlet manifold vacuum to boost the hydraulic pressure in the brake system.

Brake system - bleeding

Hydraulic fluid has to transmit pressure and it can do this only as long as it is pure fluid without air in it. Once there is air in the system, pressing the brake pedal compresses the air and does not transmit pressure through the fluid.

If the brake pedal travels to the floor, or nearly to the floor, it could be caused by one of two faults - wear of the friction material or air in the system. The way to decide which is causing the trouble is to pump the pedal several times to decrease the amount of travel, then press the pedal very firmly. If the pedal feels solid, the cause of the excess travel is wear on the linings. The simple cure for this is adjust the linings using the adjusters on the brake back plate (see drawing). Ideally remove the drums, clean out the dust and inspect the linings before adjusting the brakes.

If the pedal feels spongy when it is depressed rather as if there were a rubber ball beneath the pedal, then there is air in the system. First investigate how the air got into the system. Check every connection for signs of fluid loss, removing the drums and examining the wheel cylinders as well. There are only two ways of air getting into the system; having a faulty connection or cylinder, or ignoring regular topping up of the master cylinder reservoir. If there isn't an obvious cause of air getting in seek specialist advice - if air can get in, fluid can get out and this could leave the car without brakes.

If it is found that the fault is due to air, the brakes will need to be bled. This process replaces the fluid in the system and gets rid of all the air. Purchase a Castrol Bleedmaster kit from any leading accessory shop. If the instructions on the pack are followed implicitly the brakes will be satisfactorily bled easily in a

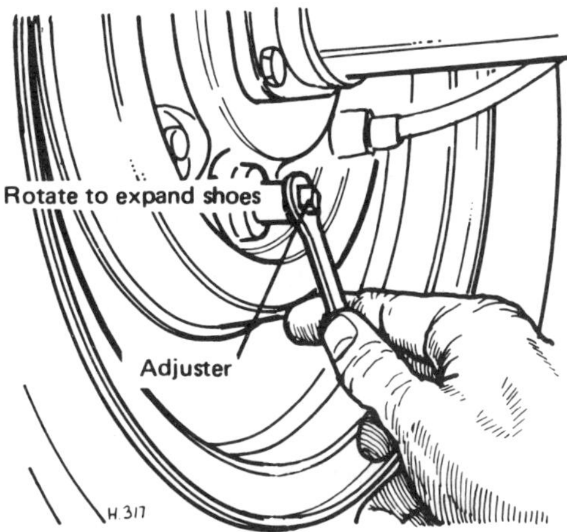

Drum brake adjustment
There are various types of adjuster used on drum brakes, so consult your handbook before starting work. Tighten the adjuster until the drum locks, then release the adjuster just enough to allow the drum to spin. There is bound to be some contact between the drum and brake lining so do not aim for a completely clear spin, just avoid any binding of the drum on the lining.

short space of time. However if this kit is not available a fresh supply of the correct brake fluid will be needed, a glass bottle or jar and a length of rubber tubing. The tubing can be obtained from any leading accessory shop.

The bleeding method is straightforward. Starting from the wheel farthest away from the master cylinder, put some clean fluid in the bottle, slide the tube over the bleed nipple and put the other end into the fluid. Slacken the nipple about three quarters of a turn and get someone inside the car to press the brake pedal three or four times, then tighten the nipple and check the level in the master cylinder reservoir. Repeat this operation until the fluid bleeding from the tube is free of air bubbles. Carry on to the other three wheels finishing with the one nearest to the master cylinder.

On no account re-use the fluid which has been bled into the bottle, as it is contaminated with water and waste particles and would only make matters worse. It is strongly recommended that the fluid bled from the braking system be thrown away immediately the operation of brake bleeding has been completed. Try to avoid shaking the fresh hydraulic fluid as this may also trap air bubbles which will then be carried into the system. After all four wheels have been bled, check pedal pressures, and if it is still spongy despite having completely replaced the fluid, the system will have to be looked at by a specialist as there is an untraced air leak present.

Hydraulic brake fluid does not only take in water in the car, it will also absorb the moisture from the air space in the brake fluid container, therefore never leave the lid off a tin of brake fluid for longer than is necessary and never get a larger tin than you need. It is best to buy fresh fluid when it is needed or have a sealed tin in the garage. As soon as a tin of fluid is finished throw the tin away, never use it for storing something else - putting anything other than brake fluid into the system could be the last mistake that is ever made.

Always use Castrol Girling Universal Brake and Clutch Fluid which is the only fluid authorised for use in most hydraulic brake and clutch systems.

Important If the braking system fitted to your car has a dual line system with a tandem master cylinder always refer to the manufacturers handbook or service instructions for the special procedures to be used for bleeding the system.

Linings and pads

Never use anything but the best linings and pads. The leading manufacturers do a lot of research and produce friction materials with excellent wear characteristics and resistance to fade due to overheating. Never change the linings or pads on one wheel only. Even if only the one wheel is contaminated by an oil leak, change the linings or pads on both sides to maintain a proper balance. A slightly different material, or one side being less worn than the other, could cause the car to pull to one side during braking, or even cause a skid.

Most owners actually use their brakes fully about once a year, for the rest of the time they are used at a third of their potential or less. Make a point of trying a full power stop about once a month, having checked the mirror first! It may not be particularly good for the tyres but it is a sure way to see if the brakes are working properly before an emergency happens. Get into the habit of applying a strong pressure to the brake pedal before starting a journey. Hold the pressure for a few seconds and see if the pedal is solid or if it moves after pressure has been applied. If it slowly moves towards the floor there is a leak or a faulty master cylinder, so investigate the cause at once.

Changing hydraulic fluid

As previously explained, braking generates heat and because brake fluid is in close proximity to the hottest parts of the system it must possess special properties to resist the effects of heating. The most important of these is a very high boiling point and that for Castrol Girling Universal Brake and Clutch Fluid is 550° F which provides an excellent safety margin.

Flexible pipes in the hydraulic system are unavoidably slightly permiable and therefore permit the ingress of water over a period of time. The presence of water reduces the brake fluid boiling point and the stage can be reached where heat generated on braking is sufficient to boil the water content, causing pockets of vapour in the hydraulic system and consequent brake failure.

It is therefore essential to change the brake fluid at regular intervals (see manufacturer's handbook) making sure to use Castrol Girling Universal Brake and Clutch Fluid.

Braking system - general lubrication

Do not forget to lubricate the handbrake linkage regularly to ensure ease of operation at all times. The brake pedal pivot point should be lubricated with a little engine oil but take care it does not drip onto the carpeting.

The suspension, steering and tyres

When a car is being driven even on good road surfaces the car body and its occupants can be subjected to three different types of motion. These are bounce, roll and pitch.

With a car travelling at speed, one or more wheels can hit a bump and bounce off the road surface for a fraction of a second.

As a result of centrifugal action when negotiating a corner the car body can be pulled away from the centre of the curve and cause the body to tilt or roll, on the road springs. In extreme cases the car can in fact roll over!

Pitch is the result of the rear wheels following the front wheels over a large bump. As the front of the car rises the rear will drop and then as the rear of the car rises over the same bump the front drops and the car will tend to pitch in a fore and aft movement.

The function of any suspension system is therefore to counteract the three forms of body motion. The way a car handles and steers is usually of next importance to engine performance to any car driven.

When a car is being driven around a corner each of the two front wheels must be free to travel on two different circles having a different radius but from a common centre. If the wheels were turned by an equal amount physical steering would be difficult and tyre wear excessive.

If a car is fitted with independent front wheel suspension the steering wheel must allow for the vertical movement of one wheel independently of the other.

The steering gear consists of a steering wheel, steering gearbox and linkage to each road wheel.

Road spring

Although there are many ways and means of coupling suspension systems they all basically rely on a spring and a shock absorber. There are three main types of road spring:
1 Leaf spring
2 Coil spring (helical spring)
3 Torsion bar

The leaf spring comprises a number of steel strips called leaves mounted one on top of another and clamped together. The most common arrangement is for the spring with the shortest leaf underneath to be bolted at its centre to the wheel axle and the two ends attached to the underside of the car body or frame.

Each end of the spring is pivoted, the rear end being connected by a swinging link known as a shackle. This method of attachment allows for the spring length to alter as it straightens out when hitting a bump. When the road wheel passes over a bump, the spring is compressed and the leaves slide over each other and then force the road wheel back into contact with the road where it returns to its normal shape.

A coil spring is a strong helical spring which is used in place of the leaf spring. It is normally fitted to front wheels to provide independent wheel suspension.

The torsion bar is sometimes used instead of a coil spring on independent suspension systems. It comprises a steel rod which is anchored at one end and twisted by the upward deflections of the road wheel. In untwisting it forces the wheel back onto the road surface.

Rubber suspension is used on at least one popular car and in this case the spring is substituted by a rubber cone. Compressed by the vertical movement of the road wheel it expands again so forcing the wheel back onto the road surface. A further development of this type of spring is employed in the 'Hydrolastic' system which uses fluid to transfer the weight of the car onto conical rubber springs.

Dampers

The function of a shock absorber is to dampen down the bouncing action of a road wheel after it has hit a bump. It also serves to dampen the oscillations of the springs.

There are a considerable number of different types of dampers but most of them operate on the hydraulic principle. They comprise a cylinder filled with a special hydraulic fluid which is transferred from one half of the cylinder to the other through a controlled orifice by the action of a piston connected to the axle. The unwanted vertical movement of the axle or wheel is therefore rapidly dampened out.

Front suspension

Almost all modern cars use independent front suspension in one form or another. Not only must the suspension allow for the rise and fall of one wheel independently of the other but it must also allow for each wheel to be turned to enable the car to be steered.

The most popular form of independent front suspension is the coil and wishbone type.

Rear suspension

The most common form of rear suspension is that which uses a pair of leaf springs and a rigid rear axle. Some cars use torsion bars, coil springs or rubber cones whilst others have a single transverse leaf spring attached at its centre to the final drive casing and a road wheel located at either end forming independent rear suspension.

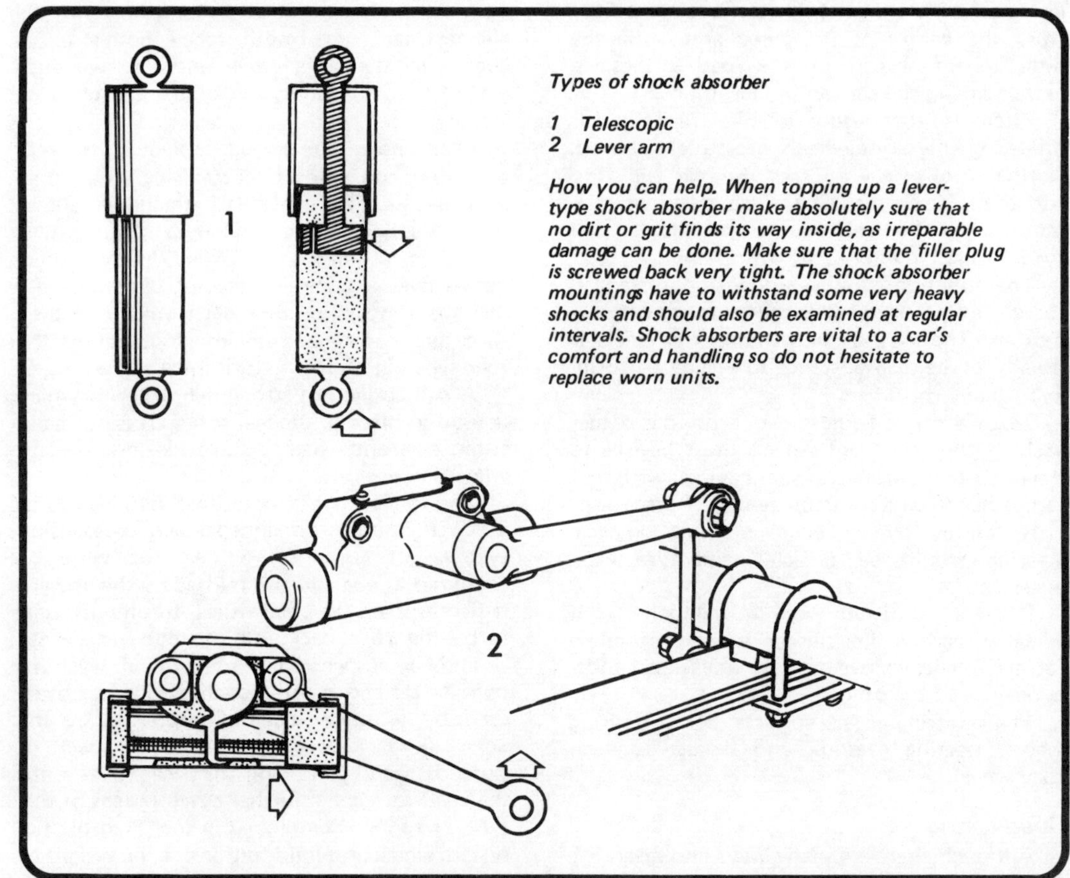

Types of shock absorber

1 *Telescopic*
2 *Lever arm*

How you can help. When topping up a lever-type shock absorber make absolutely sure that no dirt or grit finds its way inside, as irreparable damage can be done. Make sure that the filler plug is screwed back very tight. The shock absorber mountings have to withstand some very heavy shocks and should also be examined at regular intervals. Shock absorbers are vital to a car's comfort and handling so do not hesitate to replace worn units.

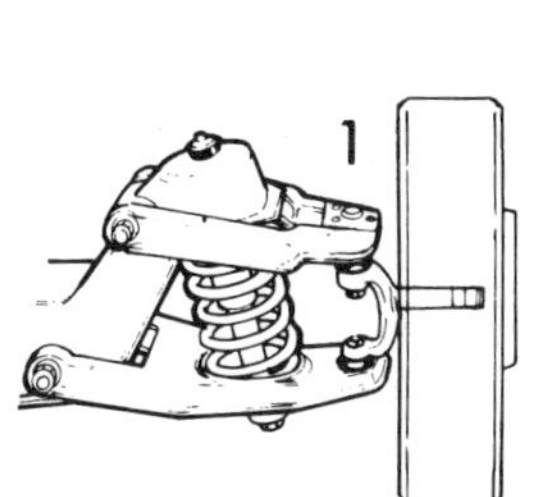
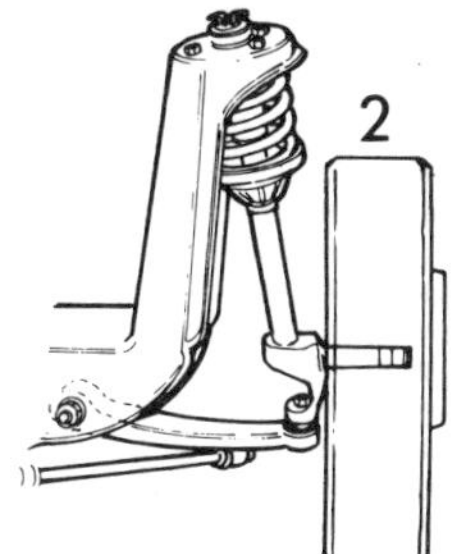
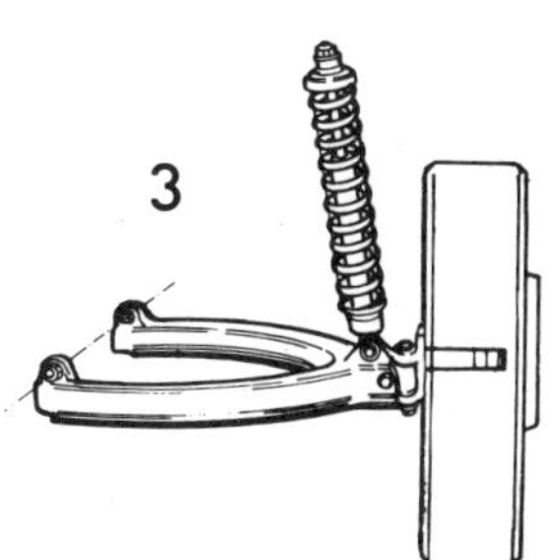

Types of front suspension

1. Wishbone and coil spring
2. MacPherson strut
3. Lower wishbone plus coil
4. Torsion bar

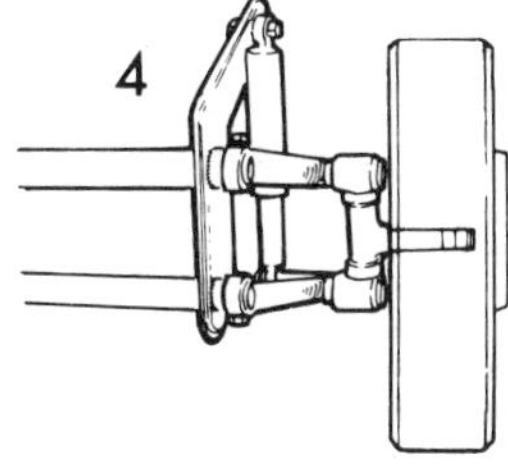

Carefully follow the maker's instructions for maintaining the type of suspension that your car employs. The modern tendency is to fit self-lubricating bushes or rubber inserts all round. Keep these clean and, if a squeak develops, add a touch of brake fluid — NOT lubricating oil as this perishes rubber. Where grease nipples are fitted, clean them thoroughly before greasing. It is important that all points should be lubricated at the correct intervals. Have the suspension geometry checked at least every 5,000 miles for wheel alignment

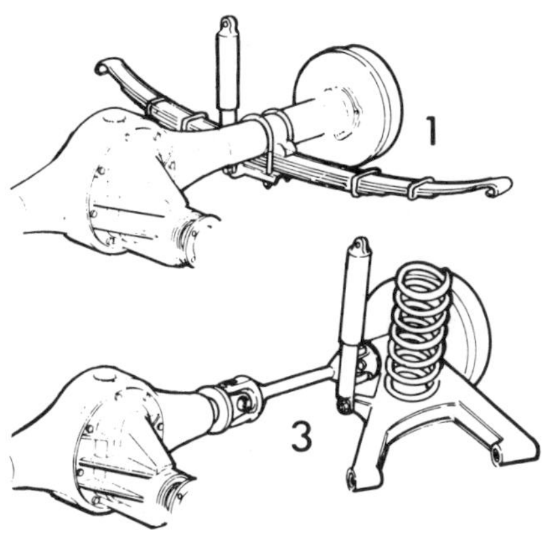
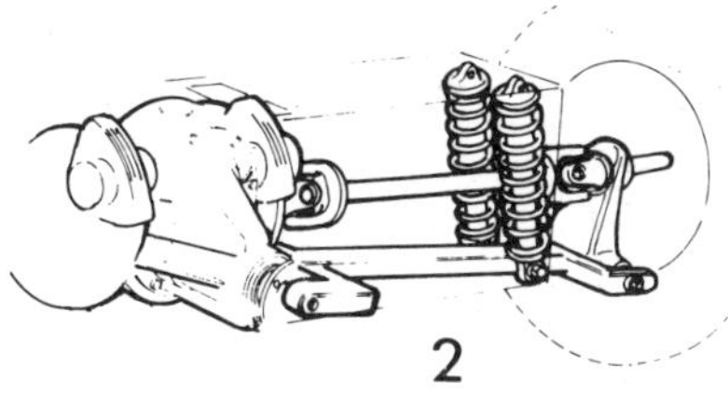

Types of rear suspension

1. Leaf spring
2. Parallel link
3. 'A' bracket
4. Swing axle

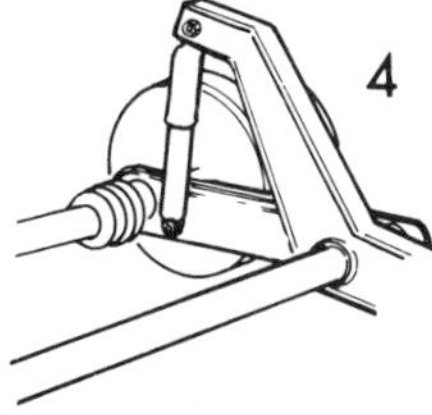

How you can help. Simple leaf suspension requires very little attention. Keep leaves clean and, if recommended in the handbook, lubricate occasionally with Castrol Penetrating Oil. Treat shackles with the recommended Castrol lubricant. Do not forget the propeller shaft bearings (however difficult they may be to get at!), and always use water-repellent greases such as Castrol LM or MS3 Grease. In rainy weather grease more frequently.

Steering

The steering wheel is attached to the end of a tubular shaft which is enclosed in a fixed tube called the steering column.

The rotary movement of the steering wheel is converted to a lateral movement by either a steering box or simple rack and pinion assembly.

The steering box comes in many forms but one of the more popular is the recirculating ball type. This design resembles that of a worm with coarse pitch helical grooves of semicircular cross section and a nut. The outer ends of the groove in the nut are joined by a bolt on steel tube which completes a path for the free-running steel balls with which the nut groove is filled. The cross shaft carries a peg which is engaged with a hole in the side of the nut. As the worm is rotated, the nut is wound up or down the worm and the balls pass around their circuit. The only contact between the nut and worm is made through the point contact of the balls and friction is therefore low.

When the nut moves up or down, the cross shaft is rotated and so creates movement in an operating arm which is attached to the outer end.

One half of the operating arm is connected to the offside road wheel by a short track rod and the other half to a long track rod which runs across the underside of the car to one leg of a second operating arm on the nearside of the car.

This second operating arm is carried on the shaft of a steering idler. The other leg of the operating arm on the steering idler is connected to the nearside road wheel.

The rack and pinion steering operates on a different principle. A pinion is attached to the end of the steering shaft and engages with a rack connected to the road wheels through tie rods and balljoints.

When the steering wheel is turned the pinion moves the rack one way or the other and the balljoints allow for independent rise and fall of the road wheels.

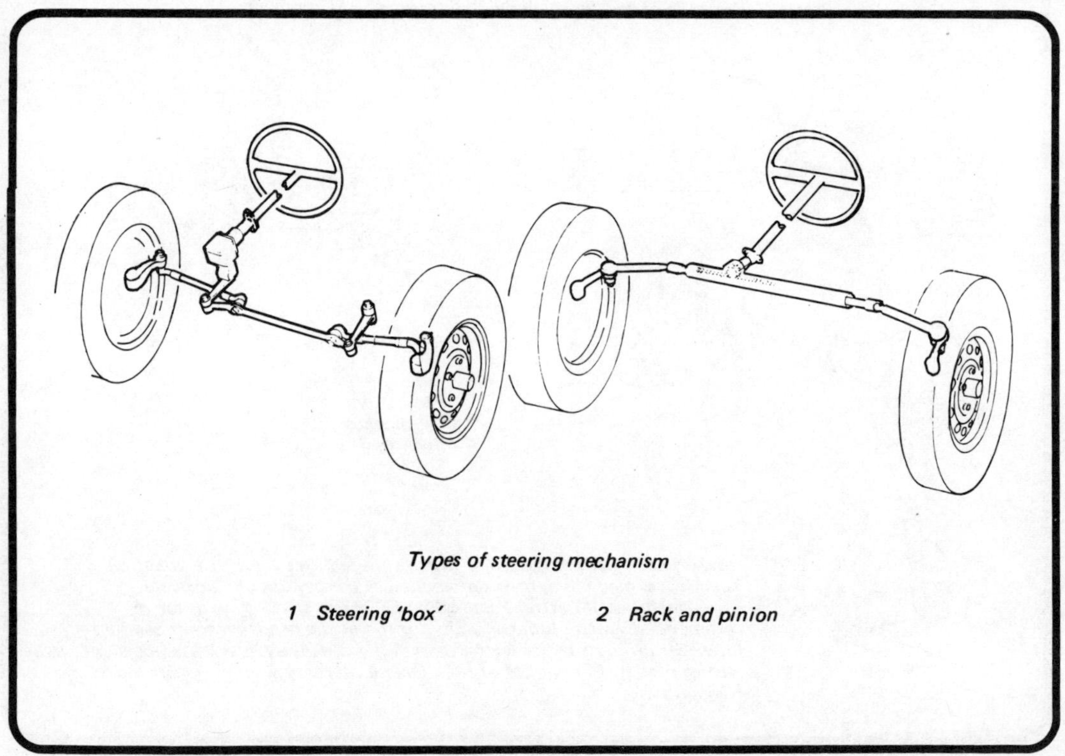

Types of steering mechanism

1   Steering 'box'   2   Rack and pinion

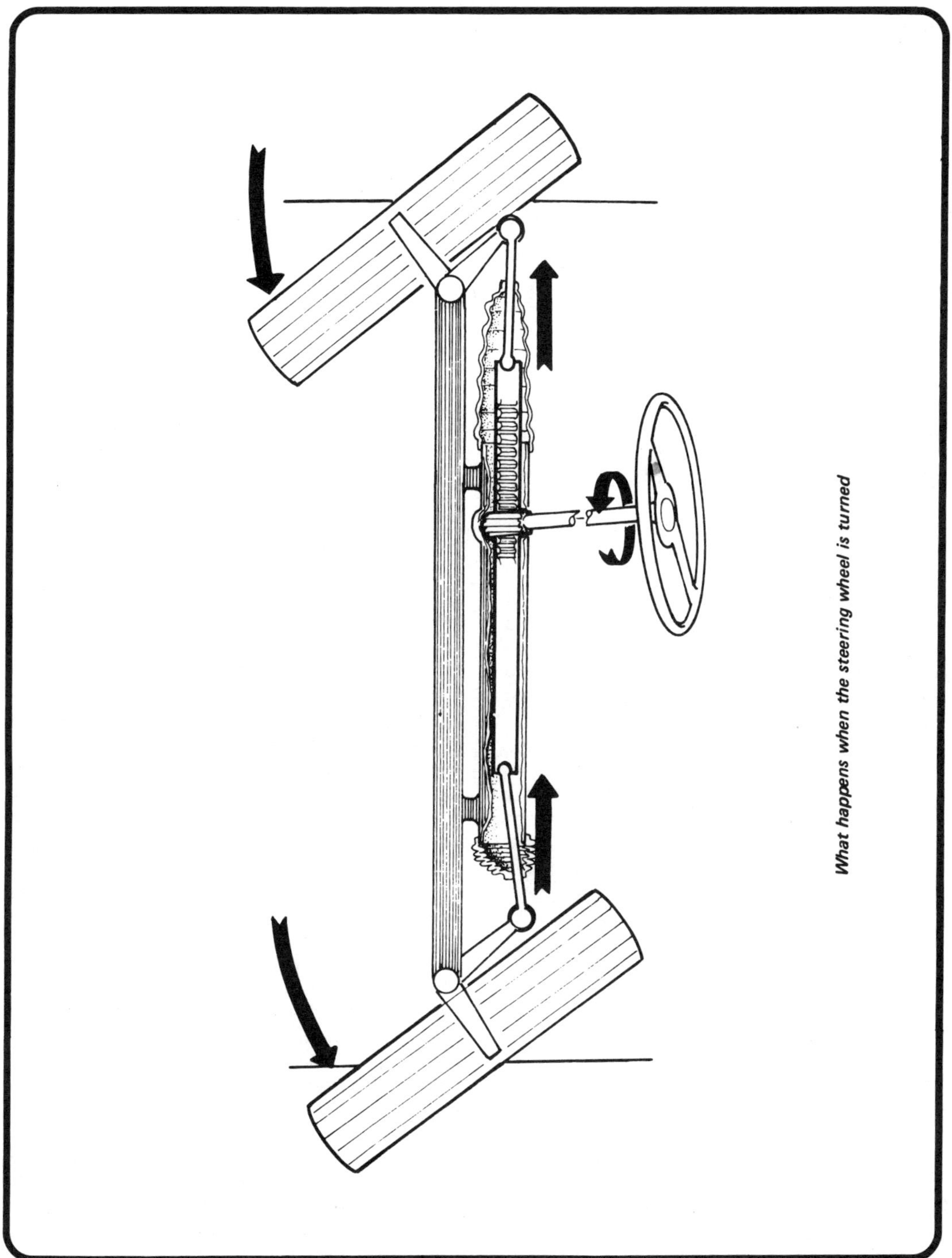

What happens when the steering wheel is turned

Tyres

All the loads of braking, accelerating and cornering are fed into the car by the tyres. They have a vital part to play in safe motoring. If the tyre looses its grip on the road then the car is virtually out of control. Make a regular check on the tyre pressures, tread depth and wall condition.

Maintenance of correct tyre pressures is extremely important to tyre grip and life. The pressures recommended for the tyres are those which will give enough flex to have some cushion effect, but not enough to allow the tread to distort or cause excessive heat built up. An over-inflated tyre will give a harsh ride as there will be virtually no give in it and the centre of the tread will wear out quickly because the extra pressure will not allow the tyre to settle down on the road. An under-inflated tyre will destroy itself fairly quickly due to heat build up, because if the tyre can move about because there is insufficient pressure to hold it properly in shape, there will be rapid build up of heat from the flexing of the tread and walls. Too high a temperature will soften the tyre rubber, allowing it to flex even more, thus causing more heat....Finally the inner bracing starts to part from the rubber and the tyre gives up.

Check tyre pressures at least once a week. The greater the mileage the more often should the pressures be checked and certainly before any long journey. It is unwise to rely on the normal garage pressure gauges which are used and misused by anyone. The wise owner purchases his own pressure gauge from a good accessory shop and treats it carefully. Don't experiment too much with tyre pressures, because the vehicle and tyre manufacturers did a lot of work to come up with their recommendations. Generally do not exceed four pounds per square inch either side of their recommendations.

Regularly check the walls of the tyre for bulges or splits. This is one advantage of wheel rotation. Taking off the wheels every 6000 miles and moving them to another corner does give the chance of regularly checking the inside wall of the tyre and also pick out all the jammed-in sharp stones. Rotating the tyres does increase their useful life.

Tread depth on a tyre is what controls water dispersal. The tyre uses the friction between itself and the road to transmit all the forces of car control, and if water can establish a film between the tyre tread and the road it substantially reduces the friction to a point where there is little or no grip at all. To prevent this happening, a tyre tread is designed such that the raised sections of the tread force the water into the channels between the raised sections and out to the rear. These channels can be considered as pipes - the bigger the pipe the more water it will carry. When the tread cannot get rid of the water quickly enough, it builds up in front of the tyre and forms a wedge which the tyre rides up, and hey presto - lubrication, no friction, and no control either. This effect is known as aquaplaning and happens when a car is driven with very shallow treads or too fast on a badly waterlogged road. This is why there is a road traffic act making it an offence to drive a car with less than one millimetre of tread depth. This is an absolute minimum, and many experts consider a tyre with two millimetres of tread to be worn out. Once control of a car is lost in the wet, the driver has to be a real expert to regain control, always providing something isn't hit first.

There are two types of tyre commonly in use, cross-ply and radial-ply, and the difference in their construction gives them very different characteristics. The cross-ply has a uniform bracing section which goes round the tread and walls. It retains its shape over bumps and camber changes so that an area of tread can be out of contact with the road if the angle of the road wheel opposes the road camber.

The radial tyre, on the other hand, has a lightly braced, flexible wall with a heavily braced stiff tread. This means that changes in camber of wheel angle can be taken up in the walls and the tread remains firmly on the road, giving a better grip between the tyre and the road.

The radial-ply tyre lasts longer than the cross-ply because the tread area is maintained in maximum contact and therefore the wear is shared out evenly. It is not quite the panacea for all ills that many would make out - it gives a harsher ride and transmits more road noise than a cross-ply tyre, and when it finally breaks away it does so with little warning.

Whichever type of tyre you choose, remember that they must not be mixed. Although the law permits the use of cross-ply tyres on the front two wheels and radials on the rear, it is not recommended. It gives rise to some peculiar handling characteristics, especially to cars which tend to understeer anyway. The other snag is that unless two spare wheels are carried, the driver risks a driving licence endorsement should there be a puncture.

To drive with cross-ply and a radial-ply tyre on the same end of the car is an offence. For safety's sake use a complete set of tyres of the same type.

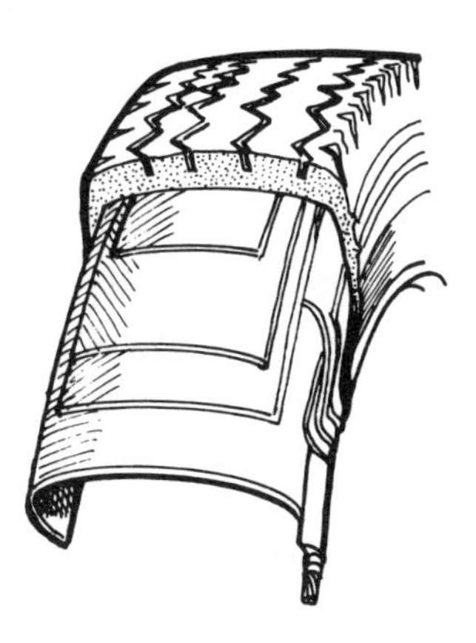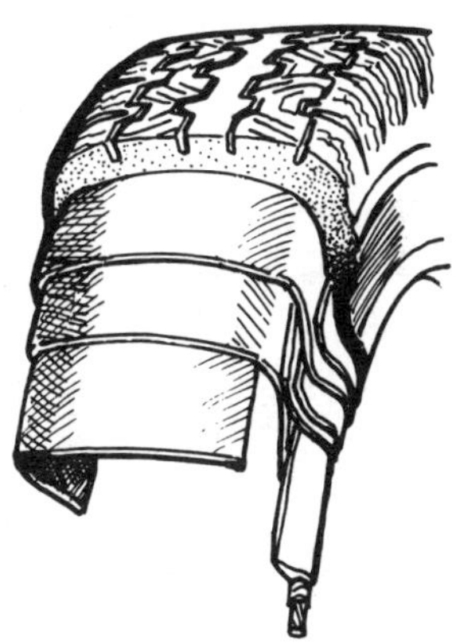

Tyre construction — a cross section of a cross-ply (left) and radial ply (right) tyres

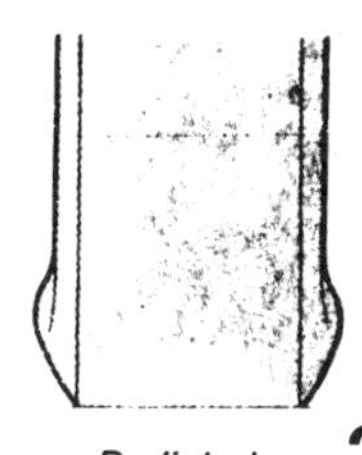

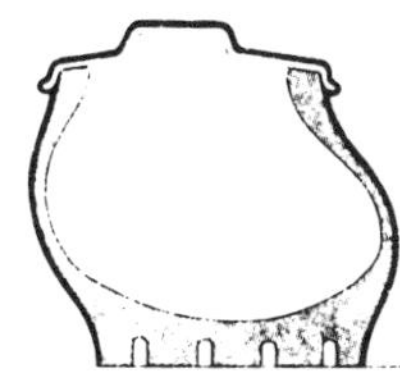

Cross ply and Radial ply tyres
The difference in the construction of the two types of tyre gives them very different characteristics. The cross ply (1) has a uniformly strong tread and wall bracing. This gives it better cushioning properties but allows some deformation on bad surfaces and cambers. The radial ply tyre (2) has a supple wall and a firmly braced tread, ensuring that the maximum area of tread is kept in contact with the road despite suspension angle changes and road camber effects.
On no account should the two types of tyre be mixed on the same axle.

The spare

The spare tyre could be considered to be the most important tyre on the car. There may never be a need to use it, but if there should be a flat and no spare, the time and trouble it takes to get the car moving again is infuriating. There could also be trouble on a motorway where summoning help usually results in a large bill.

Keep a regular eye on the spare, checking its pressure with those of the other wheels. If it losses pressure between checks, have it examined by a tyre specialist. There is no point in replacing one flat tyre with another which will go down in a very few miles. So always carry a good spare.

If the car has very different tyre pressures front to rear, always inflate the spare to the higher of the two pressure. It is easier to let out air to correct the pressure, but there may not be somewhere where air can be put in.

Lubrication maintenance

Most modern cars are now fitted with sealed rubber or nylon suspension joints but always check in the manufacturers handbook to see if there are any external lubrication points. If there are these must be regularly lubricated otherwise the steering will become stiff and un-responsive as well as increasing wear in the steering and suspension joints.

Do not forget that in most steering boxes there is an oil filler plug for topping up the oil level.

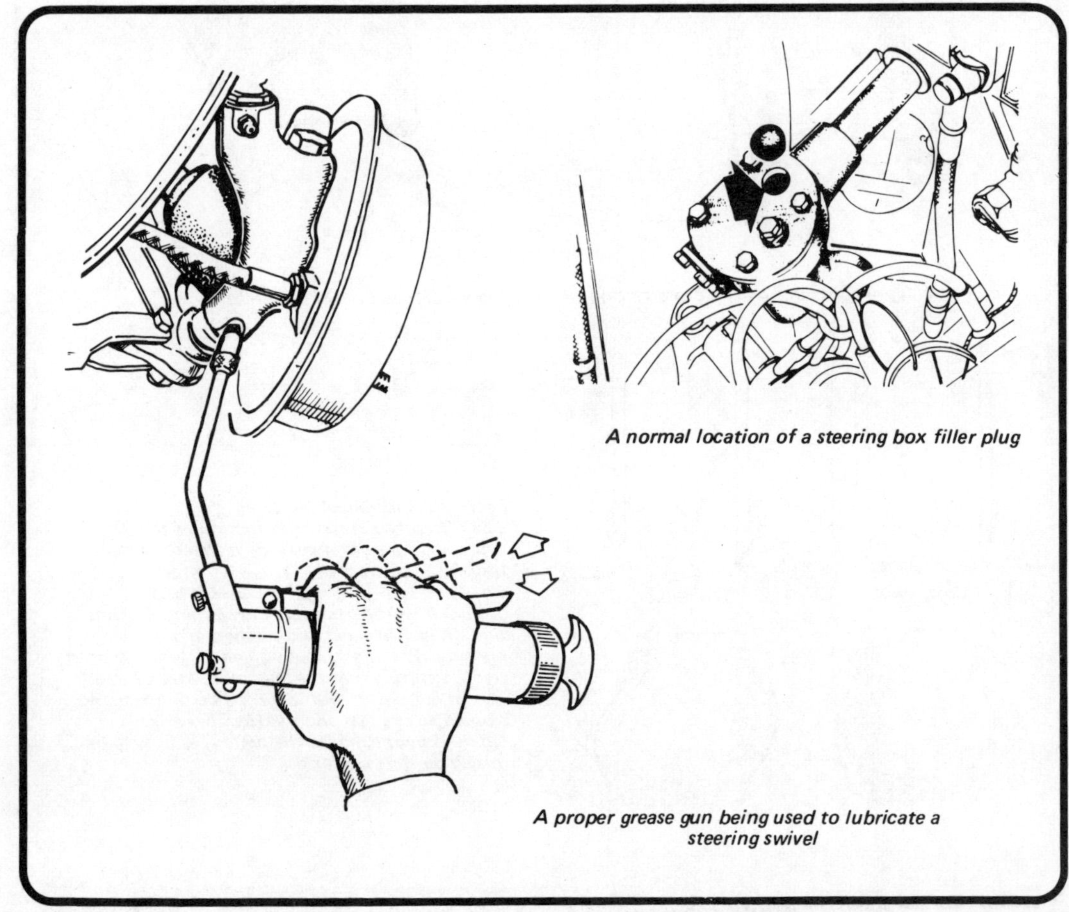

A normal location of a steering box filler plug

A proper grease gun being used to lubricate a steering swivel

The electrical system

The electrical system has a vital part to play in the modern car. It supplies the power to start the engine, the sparks to keep the engine running and it operates many other devices such as wipers, horn, lights, direction indicators, heater blower and various accessories fitted to the car.

The heart of the system is the battery which can be considered as a reservoir of electrical power. A drain is put on this reservoir whenever the car is started, left parked with the lights on or when any electrically operated equipment is used.

To refill this reservoir the car is fitted with a charging system which converts a small part of the engine's mechanical power into electrical power.

The engine drives a generator, either a dynamo or an alternator, via the fan belt, providing power to run the car's electrical equipment and to recharge the battery.

Two basic maintenance jobs will help to ensure the proper functioning of the system. These are regular checks on the level of the electrolyte in the battery and of the tension and condition of the fan belt.

The battery should be checked weekly and the electrolyte level maintained at one eighth of an inch above the battery plates. If topping-up is necessary, use only distilled water. Failure to maintain the level may cause the plates to buckle thus damaging the battery and reducing its life. Care should be taken to avoid overfilling as this will lead to spillage when the engine is running and, as the electrolyte is acidic, it will damage the car's bodywork.

The condition and tension of the fan belt should be checked at regular intervals - when carrying out a routine service is a good time. A loose or worn fan belt will slip and will not drive the generator or alternator properly, resulting in insufficient output to run the electrical system and to recharge the battery. The power to run the electrical system will then

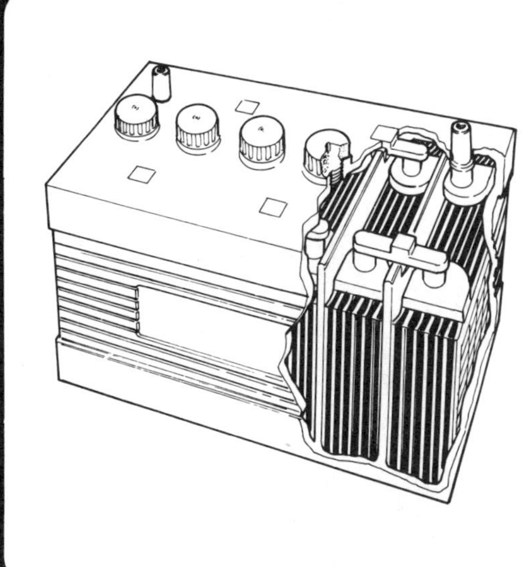

A battery cross-section
The battery will continue to work well if it is properly maintained. The level of the electrolyte (a mixture of water and sulphuric acid) should be checked once a week. If it is low, top up with distilled water until the internal plates are covered by an eighth of an inch. Do not overfill as this will lead to spillage when the engine is running. If the battery seems to use too much water between topping up (tops of the plates very dry in a week) have the charging rate checked. Also clean the battery terminals regularly and smear them with petroleum jelly before fully tightening them.

be drawn from the battery which will drain until it is completely 'flat' and the car will neither start nor run.

It is also a wise idea to remove the battery every six months, cleaning the battery carrier with a solution of bicarbonate of soda to neutralise any acid spillage, and painting the area before refitting the battery.

Apart from checking the tension of the fan belt, the only other attention required for the generator is a few drops of light oil in the end bearing every 6000 miles. Do not attempt to lubricate an alternator without prior reference to the handbook.

You will soon tell if the charging system is not giving adequate output, but it is also possible for too much output to be delivered. This will show by a drastic loss of electrolyte between checks. If this happens, have the regulator adjusted by a specialist, because overcharging will distort the battery plates causing permanent damage.

Main electrical components

Fuses and make sure that you carry at least one spare of each.

Headlamps Most modern cars have highly efficient 'sealed beam' headlamps. When failure occurs, either the wiring will be at fault or the unit will need replacing. With older cars always carry a spare bulb and keep the reflectors clean. Have the alignment of the headlamps checked regularly.

Sidelamps These are vital for your own safety and for that of other road users. Every time you take the car out you should check that they are working properly. Carry spare bulbs and make sure you know how to install them.

Stop lamps Again it is very important that these safety devices should be working all the time. If you have nobody to help you, test them at night time by reversing the car close to a wall, then press the brake pedal and look for the reflection in the rear view mirror.

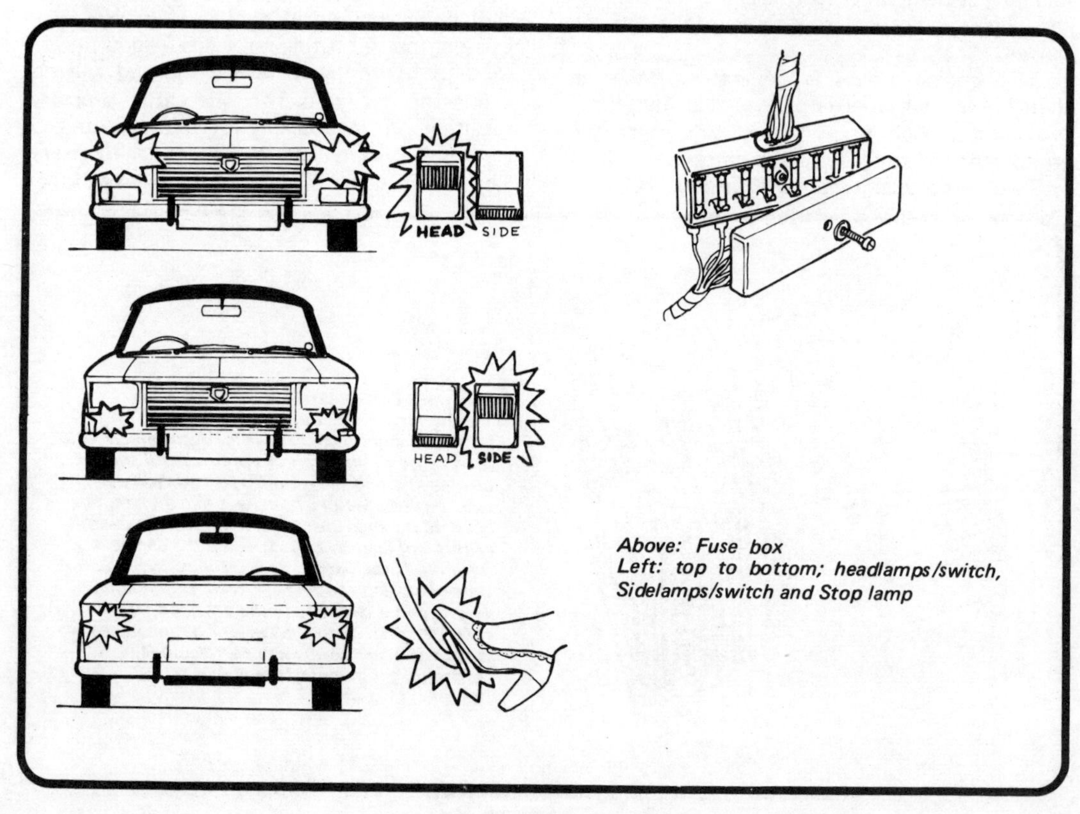

Above: Fuse box
Left: top to bottom; headlamps/switch, Sidelamps/switch and Stop lamp

Interior light It will pay you to treat this very gently! If it stops working check the automatic door plunger switches and the manual switch adjacent to the light and, of course, the bulb.

Warning lamps Because of the difficulty of testing these accurately you should not rely on them more than you can help. If you aim to keep the car a long time it is worth investing in supplementary instruments which will tell you the whole story.

Horn The instrument itself has a comparatively easy life and is unlikely to fail. Because of this, the wiring and switch gear tend to be overlooked during overhauls. Check that the horn mounting bracket does not shake loose, and keep the electrical connections clean and secure.

Instruments With the exception of the speedometer, mileometer and oil pressure gauge, most of the car's instruments are worked electrically. Sound wiring and secure connections are all important to ensure correct working. It is easier to replace faulty instruments than to attempt to repair them.

Wipers The electric wiper motor is now universal on new cars. Try to keep the load on it as low as possible by switching it off when there is no water on the screen to lubricate the blades. Most wipers are protected by a fuse, but if a motor fails a new one will possibly be needed.

Accessories When attaching electrical accessories you will usually find special electrical points provided in the fuse box, the voltage controller, and on the facia lighting switch. Always disconnect the battery before you start work. Modern heaters are relatively complicated and are best installed by skilled personnel.

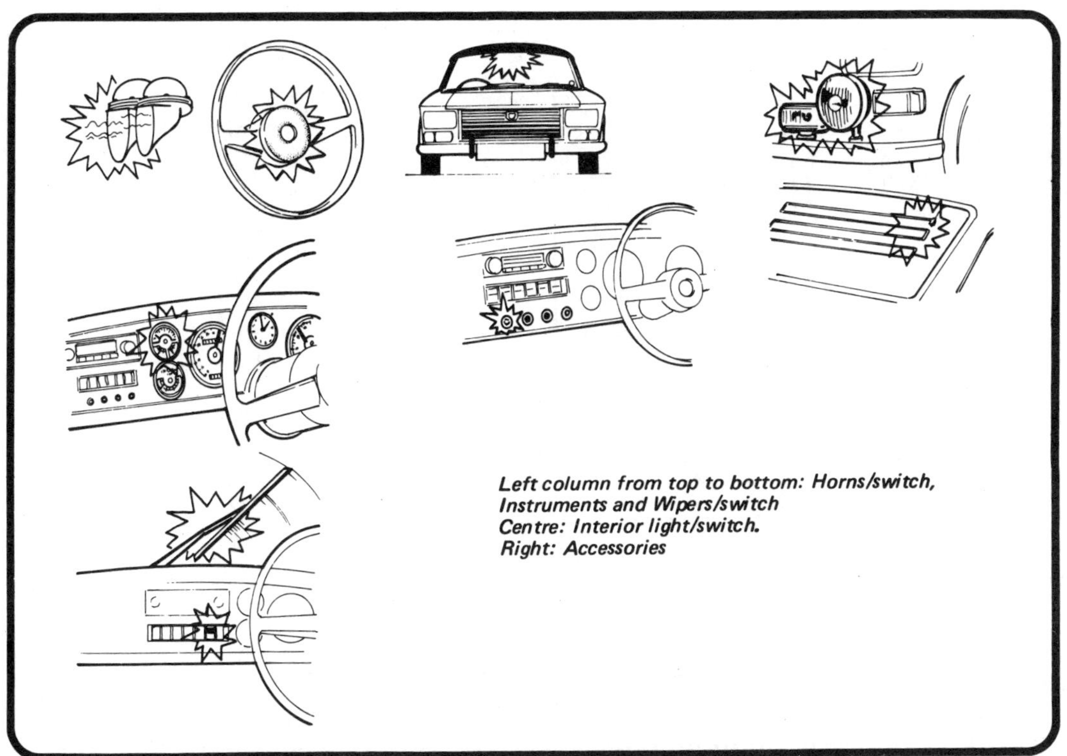

*Left column from top to bottom: Horns/switch,
Instruments and Wipers/switch
Centre: Interior light/switch.
Right: Accessories*

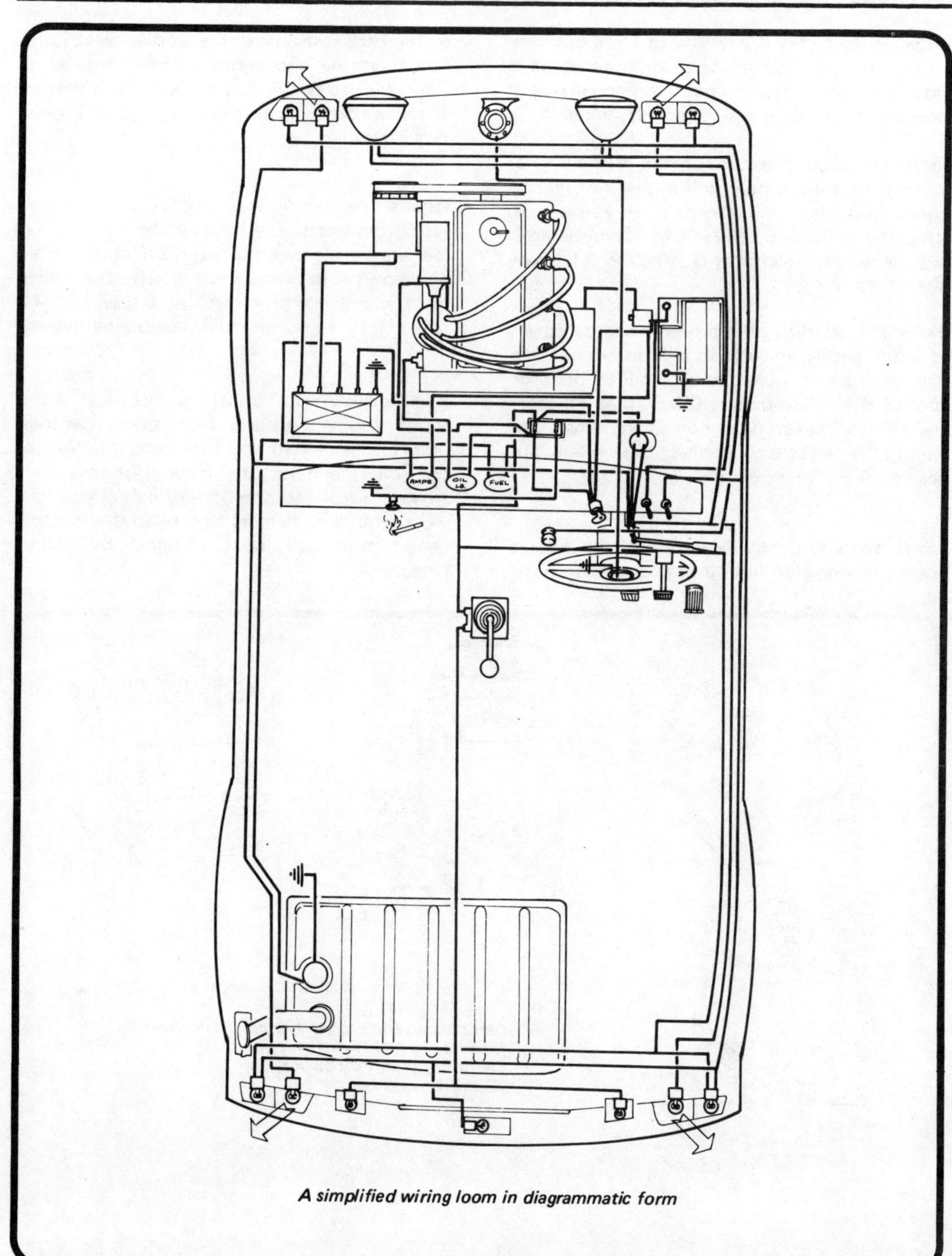

A simplified wiring loom in diagrammatic form

Routine maintenance

The modern motor car is now so advanced that designers and engineers have been able to increase considerably the period between servicing and reduce the number of items requiring attention. This has been brought about by the increase in the use of 'sealed for life' bearings, nylon bushes, better metal and lubricant technology and a reduction in the number of moving parts.

It is most important, however, that the car is still regularly serviced so that it may continue to operate at its maximum efficiency, have a long life and, of course, retain its re-sale value. The theme for servicing is prevention rather than cure so at each service interval an observant eye must be passed over the whole of the car and any small defect should be put right immediately rather than to allow it to continue to be present. Remember that any worn or damaged part will not cure itself and will, over a period of time, gradually get worse.

By following this philosophy the rate of overall wear will be kept down with the subsequent benefit of being able to keep the cost of motoring under better control.

Every car manufacturer compiles a list of items to be maintained at regular intervals and usually this is found in the handbook supplied with the car. Castrol also produce a service sheet for most popular models of cars.

Follow the sequence and do not cheat by thinking that a certain job can be done at a later date.

If the owner does not carry out his own servicing he must make sure that his car is regularly serviced as recommended by the manufacturer. When a voucher book is used it must be filled in correctly to act as a permanent record.

With any servicing carried out by the owner there are several jobs that require either special tools or test equipment. Make a list of these jobs which are applicable and then take the car to a local garage (by appointment of course) requesting that they carry out these jobs.

Many manufacturers also recommend that a seasonal check be made on the car. This is to cover different seasonal motoring conditions as well as the usual increase in summer motoring. These checks are to supplement normal routine servicing.

Just a word about safety

Accidents will happen. However, they can often be prevented. A little thought can save a considerable amount so read through the following points and always put them into practice.

1 Do not run the engine of the car in the garage with the doors closed.

2 Do not work in a garage pit with the engine running.

3 Do not wear a tie or have long sleeves when working on the engine with it running. They can easily get caught in the fan blades or fan belt. (This applies to long hair - tie it back).

4 When jacking up the front or rear of the car always chock the remaining two wheels. Where possible also apply the handbrake.

5 Do not rely on the jack to support the full weight of the car. Always supplement with axle stands or thick wood blocks.

6 Immediately wipe-up any grease or oil spilt on the floor.

7 If working under the car for any length of time ask someone to check every half an hour to make sure that all is well. Time passes slowly when trapped under a car.

8 Always use the correct size of spanner otherwise it might fly-off causing personal injury or damage to some part of the car.

9 Never use a file without a handle. The tang is pointed and very sharp. It can so easily run into the hand or wrist.

10 When drilling metal do not clean away swarf

with the fingers. Remember it is sharp - use an old clean paintbrush.

11 Do not allow battery acid to come into contact with the skin or clothes. Should this occur immediately wash off with a copious supply of cold water.

12 Do not rush a job. Before starting make sure there is ample time to finish and all the necessary tools and parts are available.

Tool kit

Before beginning to do one's own routine maintenance, or small repairs to a car, a reasonably comprehensive set of tools will be required. Although this involves quite a moderate cash outlay, in time the tools will more than pay for themselves, and if good, quality tools are purchased to start with they will last a lifetime.

Choose tools carefully, buying the best that can be afforded. British or German tools are usually made to the most exacting standards, and are of good quality metal. Although tools marked 'Foreign Made' may appear cheaper, generally they are of low quality, and consequently do not last long.

Listed is a very basic tool kit, which will suffice for normal routine maintenance and small repairs. It is a good idea to carry some of these tools in the car at all times, in case of a roadside breakdown. These tools are marked with an asterisk*. The remainder should be kept in the garage. Once routine maintenance of the car has been mastered one's confidence and ability will probably grow quickly and in time will feel able to tackle more ambitious mechanical jobs. When this time comes one can enlarge the tool kit by buying individual tools as they are required. In this way a tool kit will grow rapidly, without large bills.

Having bought some tools it pays to look after them. All that is required is an occasional wash in paraffin, followed by a wiping with an oily rag over the exposed metal sections.

Basic tool kit

Brake adjusting spanner. The type with swiveling ends is best.

*Feeler gauges. Buy the most comprehensive set available.

Grease gun. A medium sized grease gun, with a side lever action is best.

*Hacksaw. This will prove useful for removing rusted hose clips, nuts, etc. A junior hacksaw is best for work in confined spaces.

*Hammers. A ¼ lb ball pein hammer is best for general work, although a soft headed hammer will prove useful too.

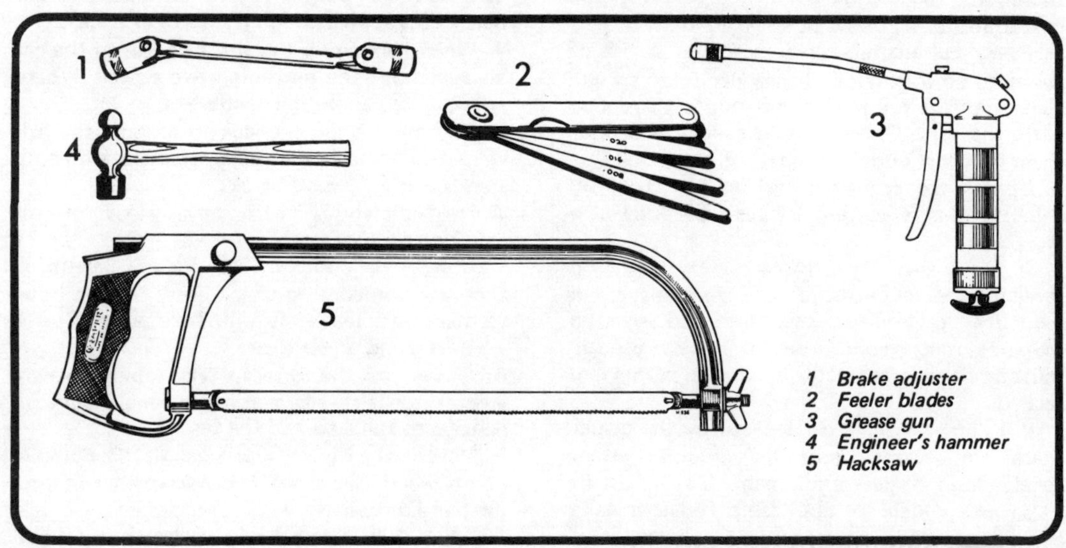

1 Brake adjuster
2 Feeler blades
3 Grease gun
4 Engineer's hammer
5 Hacksaw

Inspection lamp. The type with a caged bulb is best. Ensure the one purchased has a long wander lead and an insulated body.

Oil can. Most makes are good. However avoid those with a seam along the spout.

*Pliers. Two types are needed, 1 pair of 'Engineers combination pliers', for holding small objects and cutting/stripping electrical wire and 1 pair of 'Snipe nosed pliers' for holding small objects in confined spaces.

*Plug spanner. Choose one with a short reach and swivelling handle.

Ramps. These are not strictly necessary, but if purchased, they will prove very useful.

Screwdrivers. A selection will be needed. The following sizes and types are recommended: Engineers screwdrivers - 1 with ¼ inch blade. 1 with 3/8 inch blade and 1 medium size chubby.
Crosshead screwdrivers - 1 small, 1 medium.
Electricians screwdrivers - 1 medium size and 1 medium sized offset combination screwdriver.

When using a screwdriver, remember that its blade should be the same width as the slot in the screwhead.

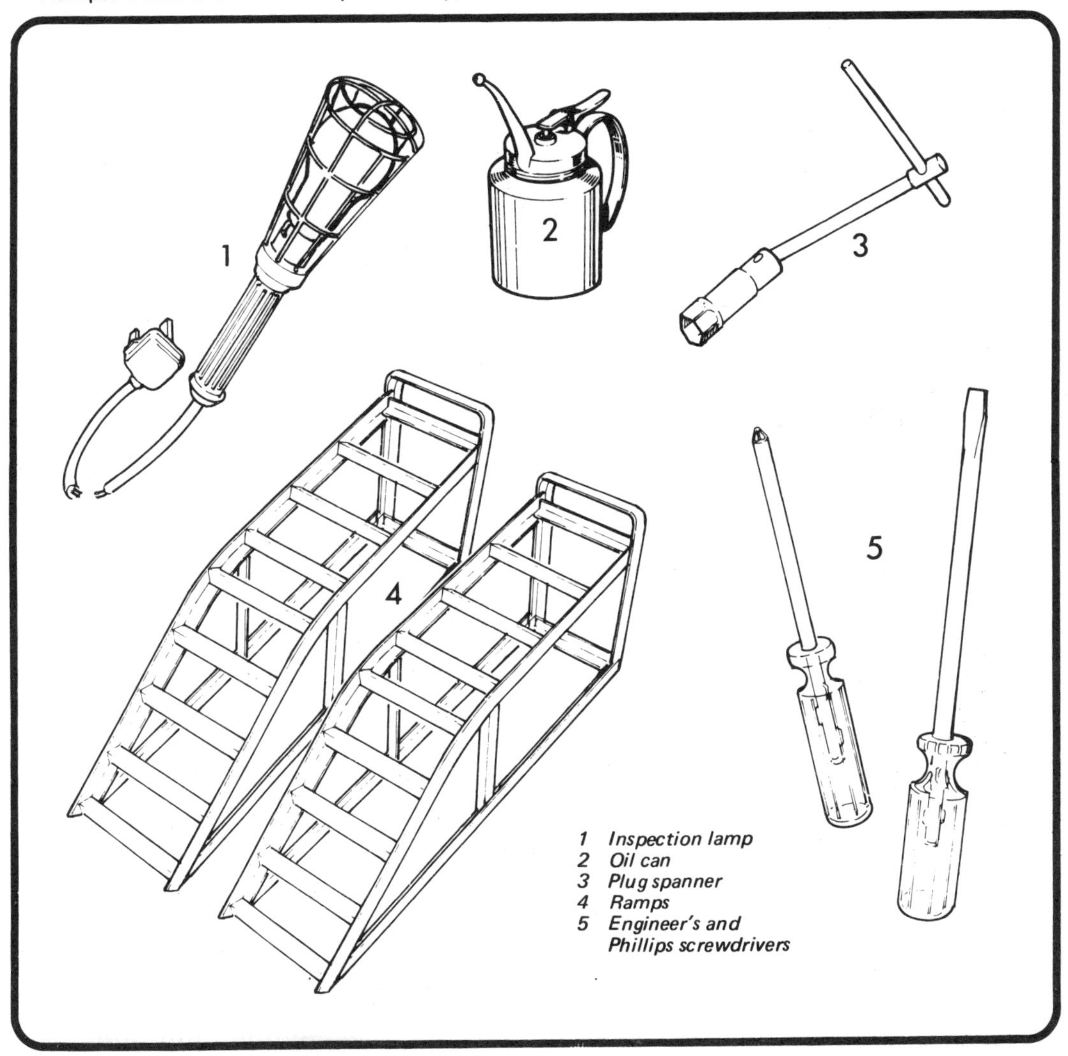

1 Inspection lamp
2 Oil can
3 Plug spanner
4 Ramps
5 Engineer's and
    Phillips screwdrivers

*Spanners. Three different types of spanner are required. They are: Open ended, the most useful for general purpose use. Ring, best for stubborn nuts and bolts as it grips the nut or bolt head around its complete circumference. Adjustable, useful for holding the nut on a bolt which is being tightened. One should never be tempted to use an adjustable spanner in place of a ring or open-ended type for fully tightening nuts or bolts, as its jaws are not completely rigid and eventually the corners on the nut or bolt will be rounded off.

The following spanners are recommended: Open-ended spanners - Buy a complete set ranging from 3/8 inch to 1/4 inch, also a set of small BA sized distributor spanners.

Ring spanners. Buy two, combining the four following sizes: 7/16 inch - 1/2 inch and 9/16 inch - 5/8 inch.

Adjustable spanners - Buy the parrot jawed type only as these are best for work in confined spaces. Buy two, one small (6 inch) for small nuts and bolts and electrical work and one medium (10 inch) for general use.

Torque wrench. Not strictly necessary, but nevertheless useful. The type with a bending shaft which moves a pointer across a scale, is both cheap and accurate. Buy one with a good range, ie 20 lb/ft - 140 lb/ft.

*Tyre pressure and tread depth gauges. Both these gauges can usually be bought as a set. The only important consideration when buying is accuracy.

Wire brush. A small one will suffice for cleaning battery terminals, earth connections etc.

Important. Before purchasing any spanners check to see which thread pattern is used for the car and obtain suitable spanners. If in doubt discuss this with a local garage.

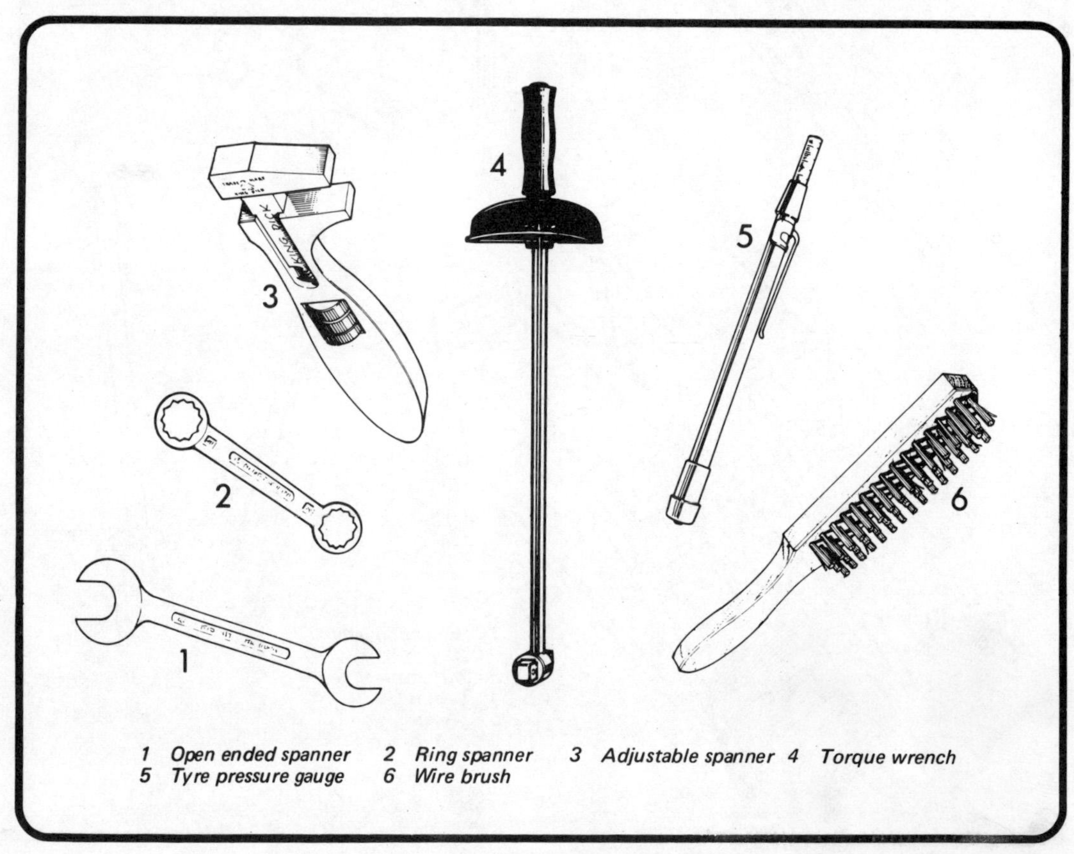

1   Open ended spanner   2   Ring spanner   3   Adjustable spanner 4   Torque wrench
5   Tyre pressure gauge   6   Wire brush

Bodywork – care and attention

Introduction

Most car owners like their cars to look clean and well polished. Not only does regular cleaning show up stone chips or rust marks which can be easily attended to before getting beyond repair, but also the appearance is maintained which helps to ensure a good re-sale value for the car.

Regular car cleaning is considered by some as a necessary evil and only to be done when absolutely necessary whilst others enjoy this aspect of car care far more than the routine maintenance of the mechanical components. The secret is to keep the car clean all the time so that it is not allowed to become too dirty making the work all that more difficult.

If the reader does not feel like doing the job all at one go then divide it into sections and do a little each periodically. This will give a continuous cleaning programme and enable other jobs to be done so breaking the monotony.

Should the car have been recently acquired and it is in a dirty state then it will be worthwhile having the whole of the underside and engine compartment steam cleaned. This will save a tremendous amount of time. It will not take long but is well worth the time.

Car cleaning - interior

Many car owners leave interior cleaning until last and prefer to wash the exterior first. This is really working backwards because the dust created by removal of carpets will only settle on the clean exterior.

By regularly cleaning the interior, the upholstery will remain in good 'nearly new' condition, the carpets fresh and clean and the general appearance smart and well cared for. When the carpeting is removed any water leaks will become evident and the necessary corrective action can be taken before rust sets in.

First empty the under dash parcel tray, rear parcel shelf, under the front seats and the luggage compartment of all the bits and pieces which have collected over the past few months of motoring, and place in a large cardboard box ready for sorting out and replacing.

Lift out the rubber slip mats, the carpeting and underfelt. The rubber mats may be washed if very dirty or just shaken to remove loose dirt. The carpeting may be brushed, shaken or beaten to remove the dust and dirt. If badly marked they can be washed using a carpet shampoo and laid out to dry in the sun. Underfelt should be carefully shaken but not washed or beaten otherwise it will be difficult to dry and may start to break up. If the carpeting around the pedals is worn renew it otherwise it can be dangerous.

Next lift out the rear seat cushion which will give better access for the next job. Using a vacuum cleaner with a flexible hose remove all traces of dust and grit.

With a suitable upholstery cleaner diluted as recommended by the manufacturer, wash down all upholstery, body trim and roof lining. Use a neat solution on stubborn stains. Wipe off all traces of cleaner or soap with a moistened cloth and finally rub dry with a clean non-fluffy rag. Do not use too much water as it will cause excessive condensation in the car unless it is a hot day, and the doors can be left open for a while.

The interior paintwork next should be cleaned using a damp cloth and polished using a domestic aerosol polish and clean non-fluffy rag. Door handles and chrome trim should be lightly rubbed with a moistened cloth.

To clean the interior glass, interior mirror and instrument glass, add a little methylated spirits to the water and wipe off with a soft cloth. Do not use ordinary domestic cleaners.

Inspect the seat belts for damage and make sure that the anchorages are still firm. The belt may be washed in warm soapy water and wiped dry with an old towel.

Wash down the door, boot lid and bonnet apertures and their edges. Remove all traces of lubricant with a paraffin moistened cloth. Take care to clean around the door hinges and locks as these are dust traps.

With a piece of wire probe the door drain holes to make sure that they are free of blockage. Inspect the floor panels for signs of rusting or leaking at the various seams. De-rust using Kurust and seal with a flexible sealing compound such as Seelastik.

Whilst the front doors are open make sure that the little courtesy light switch located in the door pillars operate freely. Check the bulb in the courtesy light for operation or for a disconnected cable at the rear of the switch if the bulb does not light.

Next go round all nuts, bolts and screws and make sure that all are tight and then lubricate the door locks and hinges, courtesy light switch plungers, choke control and front seat runners to ensure precise and free movement.

Turning to the rear luggage compartment, remove the rest of the contents including the spare wheel and vacuum out all dust and dirt. Wipe the paintwork with a moist cloth. If carpeting is fitted clean this in a similar manner to the interior carpeting. Again look for water leaks especially in the corners and if necessary seal with Seelastik once the rust has been neutralised. Clean any drain holes using a piece of wire.

Using an oil can, lubricate the handbrake lever assembly and the pedal pivot points. Inspect the pedal rubber for signs of excessive wear and fit new ones if necessary. It is dangerous to drive with worn pedal rubbers for on a wet day it is easy for the foot to accidentally slip off the pedal.

Should you have a slight tear in one of the seats or trim panel, cut a piece of spare trim from the underside of one of the seats and apply a coat of impact adhesive such as clean Bostik, insert the patch into the hole with the glue uppermost and then apply adhesive to the flap of the trim section. Allow the recommended drying time to pass and then press down the torn edges, trying to get the edges as close together as possible which will make the repair less pronounced. Any large tears will have to be repaired using a piece of matching material which should be obtainable from the local main dealer.

The time has now come for touching up the interior paintwork and full details for this will be found later in this chapter. Once the paint is dry, the rear seat cushion and carpeting may be refitted followed by the articles that live on the parcel shelf and in the rear luggage compartment.

This is a good time to check the contents of the first aid kit, if carried, and any deficiencies should be made up. Check the tools in the car tool roll and lubricate the threads of the jack. Stow away the contents of the boot making sure that the main tool kit is so situated where it will not slide around or rattle.

Car cleaning - underside

If the car is in a dirty state it is recommended that it be taken to a local garage for steam cleaning.

With the underside relatively clean it is now an easy matter to keep it clean. Remove the interior carpeting and the contents of the boot. Jack up the car as high as possible and remove the road wheels. With a garden hose, a stiff brush, tin of paraffin and scraper and, of course, suitably clad for a soaking, soak the dirt accumulated under the wheel arches and crevices, loosening where necessary with the hand scraper. This will require a lot of time and patience but working systematically, front to rear, remove dirt and oil.

Whilst the underside of the car is drying check the seams for signs of leaking. Also generally check the tightness of all visible nuts and bolts and make sure the various pipes and wires are securely clipped to the underside of the body floor panels.

Inspect the underside for signs of rusting and, if evident, clean with a wire brush and neutralise with Kurust. When the underside is really dry, seal any leaking seams with a flexible sealing compound. Wipe off the Kurust with a rag soaked in methylated spirits and apply a coat of suitable red oxide cellulose primer surfacer. Allow to dry and if the part is visible finish off with a coat of Holts car enamel spray of the matching body paint colour.

Any underbody sealer requires regular

Car cleaning and maintenance materials

1 Vacuum cleaner	2 Damp cloth	3 Duster	4 Bucket
5 Brush	6 Chrome cleaner	7 Polish	8 Seelastic
9 Leather			

10 Underseal	11 Spray paint	12 Touch-up tin	13 Touch-up pencil
14 Kurust	15 Penknife	16 'Wet and dry'	

inspection to make sure there are no loose flakes. If evident scrape off the loose area and remove any rust as described in the last paragraph. Apply a coat of red oxide cellulose primer surfacer and allow to dry. Underbody sealer is available in brush-on form, although when applied fresh at a garage it is sprayed on. A tin of this should be obtained and brushed on using a two inch paintbrush. On the wheelarches it is recommended that, because of stones being thrown up by the tyres, two coats are applied, with time allowed for drying between each coat.

Finally, before lowering the car to the ground again check the exhaust system for leaks with the engine running. Take care not to allow the engine to run too long otherwise there may be an accumulation of exhaust fumes under the car.

Car cleaning - exterior

It is recommended that once a week the exterior of the car be washed and wiped dry. For this job a flexibrush on the end of a garden hose is best, a sponge to assist wiping down and a leather to finish the operation off.

First make sure that all windows and doors are closed and place a piece of polythene sheeting over the engine and behind the grille to shield the electrics. Make sure the engine is cold first for obvious safety reasons.

Thoroughly wet the car with water using a gentle spray. Take care not to aim the jet of water directly at the windows or body seams which could start water leaks. Once the dirt has been loosened wipe down the panels using the brush with water still flowing through; this way the paintwork should not be scratched by road grit.

Next apply wax car shampoo or a little non detergent washing-up liquid, working from the roof downwards. Any stubborn dead flies, marks or tar may be removed using white spirit on a soft cloth. Do not forget to clean the wing mirrors, wiper arms and blades, radio aerial, and of course, the wheels with the hub caps removed. A leather must not be used with a detergent or shampoo as these will cause it to rot.

Finally rinse off all the suds with plenty of clean water and wipe dry using a leather. Wipe all spots and smears from the windscreen, rear screens and door glass using the leather. When the car is dry the glass may be polished with a rag soaked in a methylated spirits and water solution. Chromium plating requires regular cleaning with a damp cloth or leather. Occasionally one of the special polishes for chromium plating may be used but under no circumstances use an ordinary metal polish.

Every six months it is recommended that the exterior be wax polished. There are, however, several important points to be noted before polish is used on a car.
1 If the car is new do not polish for at least two months to allow the paint to dry fully and harden.
2 If part of the paintwork has been re-sprayed treat as if new.
3 Do not use a 'cutting paste' to remove the dull film from a car sprayed with a metallic paint.
4 When purchasing a wax polish always make sure thay it is suitable for the type of paintwork on the car.
5 Do not attempt to wax polish a car in the sun or when the body is still warm, having been in the sun. It will bake on and have to be removed with petrol.
6 Do not wax polish a car which has just been washed because paintwork absorbs moisture slightly and the wax coating can hold this moisture which can cause minute rust spots under the paint film.

Finally some don'ts to avoid deterioration of the paintwork.
1 Don't dust down or polish a dusty car. Always wash it first.
2 Don't get polish or wax on any of the glass.
3 Don't neglect hidden parts of the doors when polishing.
4 Don't allow birdlime to stay long on the paintwork - it will cause stains.
5 Don't park under trees especially in the hot sun or when raining.
6 Don't use a cutting compound or haze remover on cars finished with an acrylic paint.
7 Don't use wax without cleaning the car first.

Bodywork - paint touch-up

On any car with a steel body the greatest enemy of all is rust and this is most likely to start under the wings or along the sills because the road wheel will fling water, mud and grit onto the paint surface and it will only be a matter of time before the paint skin is penetrated and rusting starts.

It is for this reason that many new cars are given a thick coat of underseal, usually of a bituminous or rubber base. However, if this was the end of the story, paint maintenance would be relatively simple, but unfortunately it is not because chips appear at the front of the wings along the outside of the wing panels and doors as well as the edges of the bonnet and luggage compartment lid. Whilst the car is being cleaned these chip marks will again become evident and it is important that they are attended to immediately otherwise rusting will occur and spread so that what was once a small chip will gradually turn into a large area requiring a great deal more renovation work.

Touch-up paint is usually available in a touch-up pencil, a tin with a little brush in the lid, or aerosol form, and may be obtained as a good match to the original body colour. It must, however be realised that some paint colours are more stable than others. Due to the action of sunlight on an older car an exact match may be difficult.

Use a touch-up tin with brush incorporated in the lid for making good stone chips and very small scratches.

To prepare the surface for touching-up first use a silicone solvent to remove all traces of polish which will otherwise not allow the paint to adhere properly. If there are signs of rusting or the paint beginning to lift, use a sharp penknife and carefully scrape away the loose paint and rust. Then neutralise the rust with a little 'Kurust' and allow to dry. With a piece of rag soaked in methylated spirits wipe away the excess.

The prepared spot may now be touched in with the touch-up brush. Use just sufficient to touch in the area concerned. Very carefully apply a thin coat of paint only to the area concerned and allow to dry thoroughly. Apply a further thin coat of paint so as to build up to the original thickness. This will take time and patience, but with care the touch-up should be indistinguishable from the surrounding area.

Where larger areas are to be treated, again the silicone solvent will be required, but it will then be necessary to rub down the area with wet or dry paper (grade 400), using plenty of water, until the area is smooth. Again, any rust should be neutralised with Kurust.

For this type of operation it is best to use an aerosol spray, initially applying the primer. It is most important that the instructions on the canister are followed carefully, and it is always preferable to do paint jobs of this type on a warm and dry day.

If this is a first attempt at such an operation, it is a good idea to practice on an old piece of metal just to get the feel of the spray. The jet should be held 8-12 inches away from the working surface, and at right angles to it. Where a large section is to be sprayed, the work should be commenced at the centre and then progressively moved outwards.

A period of several hours should be allowed for the primer to dry and it should then be rubbed down again with the wet or dry paper. Any faults can then be rectified by applying a further coat of primer. When you are satisfied with the finish give a final rub down before applying the top coat. Here again, the same spraying technique should be adopted, but remember not to apply the paint too quickly. Two thin coats are much better than one thick one. If more than one top coat is required, the first coat should be allowed to dry overnight before any further coats. If you are spraying near chrome trim, glass or tyres, make sure that the areas not to be sprayed are properly masked with newspaper and masking tape.

Motoring at home and abroad

Before considering a long tour whether it be in this country or abroad it is advisable to thoroughly check the car and its contents. The car should be serviced early before the recommended time if necessary rather than put it off until ones return. Breakdown services, accredited dealers and spare parts are not always there when they are needed particularly abroad and in outlying districts in Great Britain.

It is recommended that when going abroad the car be given a major service at least two weeks before departure to give the garage time to carry out any major work found necessary.

Emergency pack/standard

Sooner or later even the best maintained car will break down by the roadside or refuse to start.

These breakdowns are very rarely caused by a major mechanical fault, especially with well maintained cars. Usually the fault is very minor and can be repaired in a few minutes with the correct tools, or by some ingenious use of the materials listed in the next column.

Included in this book is a fault finding section. The items in the emergency pack can be used at some stage. It is therefore a wise precaution to carry the pack in your car at all times.

Emergency pack/standard

Assorted PK (self tapping) screws, nuts and bolts.

Contact breaker points - ensure that the set purchased is the correct type for the car.

Elastic bands - half-a-dozen in assorted sizes.

Electrical wire - a yard of wire with a crocodile clip on both ends.

Emery cloth - half a sheet, fine grade.

Fan belt - ensure correct for the car.

Handbook

HT lead - one piece at least as long as the existing HT lead from the distributor to No 4 plug, with the same clips in both ends.

Light bulbs - One of each type in use on the car.

Radiator sealant - The type that comes in a pellet is the most convenient to carry.

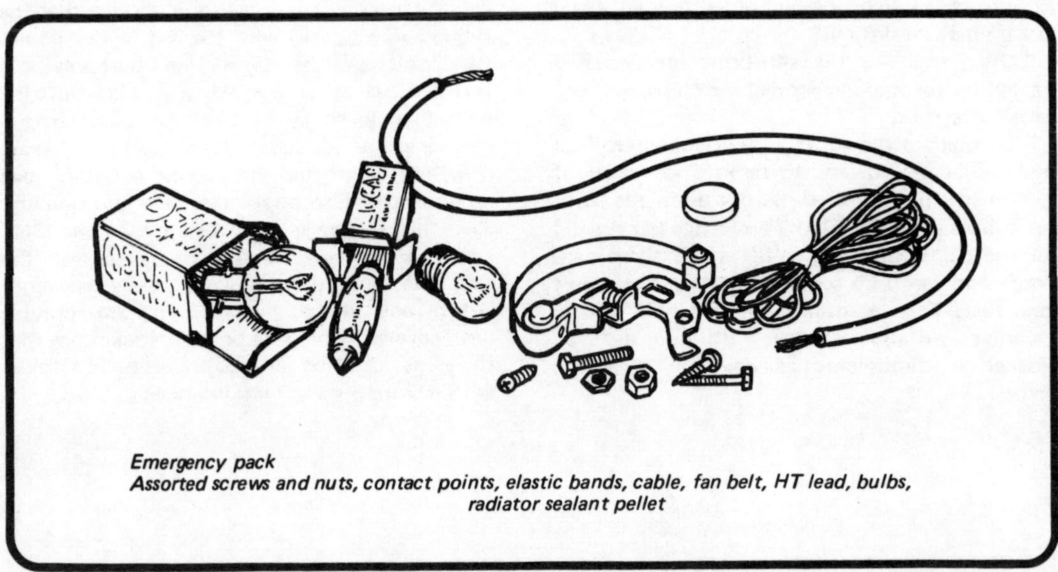
Emergency pack
Assorted screws and nuts, contact points, elastic bands, cable, fan belt, HT lead, bulbs, radiator sealant pellet

Rotor arm - Ensure the type purchased is correct for the car.

Silver paper or cooking foil - a piece of either, about 6 inches square.

Spark plug - ensure the one purchased is the correct type for the car.

String - 2 ft of strong twine.

Tape - a roll of ½ inch width plastic insulating tape.

Wire - 1 ft of thin, stiff wire will suffice.

Continental touring pack

When touring abroad it is a good idea to carry a few extra items that may be needed and difficult to get quickly in the instance of a breakdown. These items are listed below under the heading of Emergency pack/Contintental touring. Even if all the items comprising the pack are taken it is still a good idea to take out a holiday insurance, such as the AA 5 star travel scheme, which covers mechanical failure, personal injury and many other contingencies.

Some articles are obligatory when touring abroad, they include a red warning triangle, GB plate, the vehicle log book and an insurance green card. Take great care not to forget these items.

Before leaving, it is also a good idea to obtain a list of the main dealers and their addresses in the countries to be visited.

Emergency pack/Continental touring

The emergency pack detailed earlier in this section will suffice for most continental touring, However if a really long journey is envisaged, in a car which already has a high mileage recorded on the speedometer it is as well to include the following items in the pack:
Brake and clutch master and slave cylinder seals - Ensure that the seals purchased are the correct ones for your car.
Dynamo or alternator brushes.
Fuel pump repair kit
Cylinder head gasket.
Starter motor brushes.
Valve - Buy one exhaust valve only.

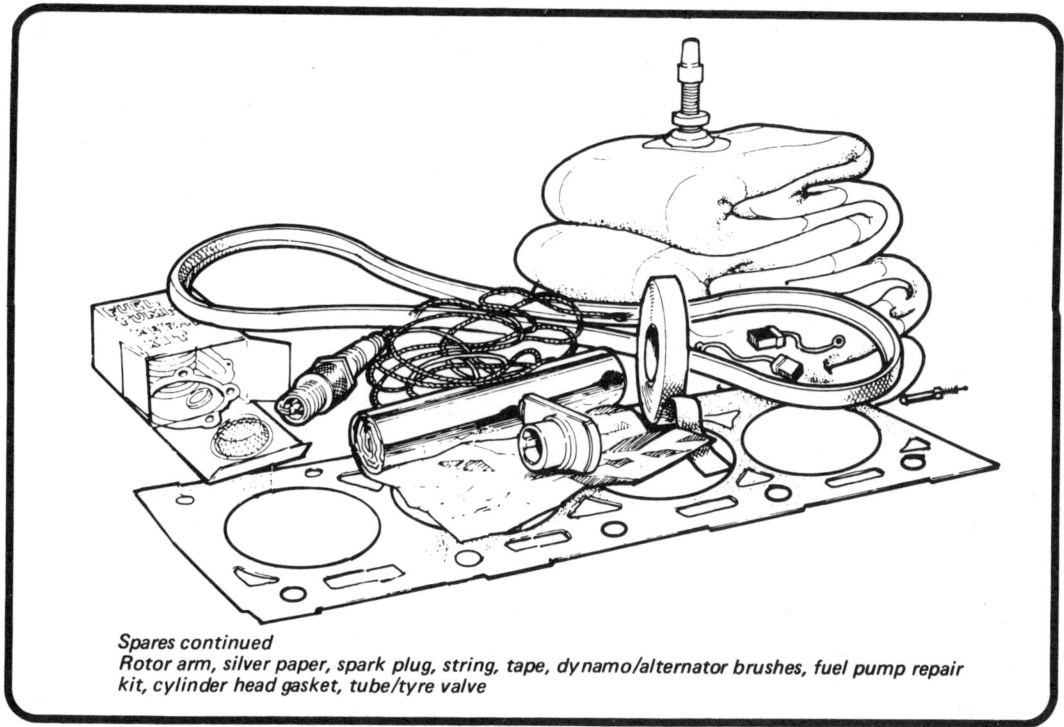

Spares continued
Rotor arm, silver paper, spark plug, string, tape, dynamo/alternator brushes, fuel pump repair kit, cylinder head gasket, tube/tyre valve

Breakdown and emergency repairs

If a car is looked after properly fault tracing should seldom be necessary because faults usually just do not happen but develop over a period of time. Possibly the car has been previously in other and less careful hands so in these circumstances the reader can inherit the results of previous neglect.

With any fault finding, the secret is to have some idea of where to start to look. In most instances this is obvious but not always so.

A careful driver is alert for signs of trouble and although none are expected if the car is not maltreated, but well maintained and correctly serviced and lubricated at the manufacturers recommended periods, any unusual noises or change in handling immediately become apparent.

Noise can tell a person a great deal, especially when unusual. With one cylinder mis-firing it will result in an uneven exhaust note which is very different from the rythmic beat of well tuned engines. If a valve clearance has slackened off the louder clicking noise from the valve gear as the excessive clearance is taken up will be obvious when the driver knows how the engine ought to sound.

It is not only the quality and location of any unusual noise but also its frequency which can give an indication as to its cause. The click of a tappet which has slackened occurs at half engine speed whereas the tapping noise of a nail in a tyre as it meets the road surface occurs at every revolution of the road wheel.

Perhaps one of the most puzzling of troubles for the driver is when the engine ceases to fire while the car is apparently running well and then refuses to restart. This can happen through a mechanical failure although it is very rare and the more common causes are due to an ignition or fuel system fault.

If the engine ceased running suddenly as if the ignition had been switched off it is probably due to ignition trouble but if the engine misfired and seemed to lose power before finally stopping, shortage of fuel in the carburettor is usually the cause of the trouble.

Fault finding therefore is based on systematic observation and logical thought. The haphazard driver who makes half a dozen adjustments to try and cure a fault may be successful without knowing which adjustment actually removed the trouble. On the other hand he can make things even worse.

When an adjustment has been made, try out its effect before moving onto the next one.

The aim of the following tables is to indicate the faults that could be encountered during a journey and the best method of rectification.

Engine suddenly ceases to fire as if switched off

Possible cause

An open circuit in either the high tension (HT) or low tension (LT) ignition system wiring.

Check and Remedy

1 Check that the ignition switch is on as it may have been accidently switched off.

2 Check for a spark:- Disconnect the HT lead from one spark plug, remove the plug cap or insert a long screw or nail and hold the end about an eighth of an inch from a paint free part of the cylinder head or block. Switch on and operate the starter motor. A spark from the head to the engine shows that the ignition system is in order.

Note: Hold the HT lead in rubber or dry cloth to prevent an electric shock.

3 Check all connections in the ignition system including the battery, switch, ignition coil, distributor and spark plugs for cleanliness and security. Do not forget the battery earth strap connection to the body and the engine/transmission earth strap.

4 Remove the distributor cap and see that the carbon brush slides freely and makes contact with the rotor arm. On some models a fixed bush is used but there is a spring contact on the top of the rotor arm.

5 Check the contact breaker arm for free movement. If it sticks with the points open then the primary circuit is interrupted.

Engine splutters, misfires, loses power and ceases to fire

Possible cause

Shortage of fuel at the carburettor or a choked jet.

Check and remedy

1 Check that there is fuel in the tank if possible using a stick or piece of tubing as the fuel gauge could be inaccurate. (This is more likely to occur when the car is climbing a steep hill with a nearly empty fuel tank).

2 Examine the carburettor float chamber for fuel. On most carburettors this entails partial dismantling but some models have a sight glass on the side. If there is fuel in the float chamber then the trouble is usually caused by a blocked jet. Dismantle further and blow out jets, clean out any sediment in float chamber and fuel passages.

3 If there is no fuel in the carburettor float chamber then either there is no fuel in the tank or there is some reason why the pump is not supplying it to the carburettor. If you hear an electric pump tick it is usually an indication that it is functioning. If the pump is mechanical try operating the priming lever, when fitted, and ensure it is securely attached to the engine. Check all unions for tightness.

4 Examine the filter in the petrol pump, in line filter (when fitted) and filter in the carburettor union (when fitted). If the pump appears to be in order, systematically disconnect each pipe in turn and blow through to clear any blockage.

5 Check all pipes and hoses for damage, corrosion, or leakage which could impede the flow of petrol to the carburettor. Any leaks can be temporarily repaired using insulating tape. Ensure that the breather hole in the filler cap is free from blockage.

Possible cause

Too rich a mixture due to evaporation of petrol in the float chamber.

Check and Remedy

Slowly depress the accelerator pedal and keep fully depressed while the starter motor is operated. This will ventilate the induction manifold and cylinders and so dilute the rich mixture. It will also bring cooler petrol from the tank to the carburettor float chamber.
As soon as the engine starts, release the accelerator.

Engine which normally runs cool rapidly overheats and cooling water boils

Possible cause

Insufficient water in radiator, broken or slack fan belt, partially blocked hose or radiator, defective radiator pressure cap or thermostat, formation of ice in the bottom of the radiator in very cold weather.

Check and Remedy

1 Examine radiator or expansion chamber (when fitted) water level.
Important: Never remove the pressure cap until steam has ceased to appear and then remove only with a large wad of cloth to prevent scalding. Never add cold water until the engine has cooled down.
2 Examine the water hose connections for leakage and the radiator itself. A leaking hose can be temporarily repaired using insulation tape. A leaking radiator can often be temporarily repaired by using some chewing gum.
3 Examine the water pump for leakage at the spindle gland. If evident a replacement pump will have to be fitted.
4 Check the fan belt tension and adjust if slack. A general guide is ½ inch deflection at the centre of its longest run. If the fan belt has broken a nylon stocking can be used as an alternative.
5 A defective thermostat which remains closed will cause overheating by preventing the circulation of water. This is usually located at the top of the cylinder head and should not be removed until a replacement can be fitted.
6 If the pressure cap seal or spring has failed the cap should be renewed at the earliest opportunity.
7 If there is no obvious cause for overheating the radiator may be badly furred up although this usually only occurs to the older car. There are proprietary preparations available for cleaning radiators and must be used according to the instructions on the pack. Always use rain water for topping up the radiator in 'hard' water areas.
8 During very cold winter days, if antifreeze has not be added or if not up to the required strength, ice can form in the lower part of the radiator when starting off with a cold engine. Stop the car until the ice has melted and blank off the lower part of the radiator with a piece of cardboard.
9 Other causes of overheating can be due to incorrect carburation, retarded ignition timing or lack of engine oil.

Engine runs normally up to a certain speed and then cuts out. It picks up again when accelerator is released

---

Possible cause

Fuel flow to the carburettor partially blocked.

Check and Remedy

See the instructions given in fault finding the second diagnosis.

Persistent spitting back through carburettor

Possible cause

Inlet valve clearance incorrect, broken or weak valve spring, sticking inlet valve, incorrect ignition timing, carburettor setting too weak.

Check and Remedy

1 Remove the air cleaner and with the engine running slowly insert a little thin oil down the air inlet. If an inlet valve is merely sticking in its guide this will usually effect a temporary cure. The remedy is to remove the cylinder head and recondition.
2 If the inlet valve clearance is too small this can cause the trouble. Reset the valve clearance (where possible).
3 A weak or broken inlet valve spring can be the cause and a replacement set should be fitted.
4 When the ignition timing is too far retarded there can be persistent spitting back in the carburettor and usually accompanied with loss of engine power. Reset the ignition timing by slightly advancing using the knurled screw usually fitted on the side of the distributor body.
5 On some carburettors it is possible to adjust the various jet settings throughout the whole engine speed range. This is a job best left to the experts. On fixed jet carburettors ensure that all jets and fuel drillings are clear of obstruction.

Engine runs but with a regular misfire

Possible cause

A dirty or defective spark plug, detached spark plug lead or dirty plug cap.

Check and Remedy

1 Upon inspection it will be apparent if a spark plug lead has become detached from the plug cap, the plug cap detached from the spark plug or the lead from the distributor cap.
2 With the ignition switched off moisten a finger and quickly touch each spark plug in turn. The defective spark plug will be cooler than the remainder.

3 Alternatively short out each spark plug or detach each plug cap in turn with the engine idling. This will have no effect on the defective spark plug and the engine will continue to run with a regular misfire.
4 Remove the faulty spark plug, clean it, reset the gap and replace it. If the trouble still exists fit a new spark plug.

Engine runs but with a irregular misfire

Possible cause

Incorrect contact breaker points gap, tracking in the distributor cap, loose cable connection in the ignition system.

Check and Remedy

1 Remove the distributor cap and check the contact breaker points gap. Reset to the manufacturer's setting.
2 Examine the cap interior for a black hair-line crack running from one or more segments. A temporary cure may be made by scratching the crack with a penknife or screwdriver until all traces of black are removed. It will at least get you home when a new cap must be fitted.
3 Check the cleanliness and security of all cables and connections in the ignition circuit.

Apparent loss of oil pressure

Possible cause

Lack of oil in sump, oil pressure gauge or switch failure, engine internal fault.

Check and Remedy

1 Immediately switch off engine and stop the car.
2 Check the oil level and top up to the correct level with the correct grade of oil.
3 Check the reason for loss of oil. Bad maintenance or oil leak? If a gasket is leaking try tightening the attachment: For example the rocker cover gasket or mechanical fuel pump.
4 It is not uncommon for the pressure switch to fail. Test the bulb by shorting the lead from the switch to earth and if the bulb lights the switch is probably at fault.
5 If no apparent cause can be found start the engine and drive carefully to the nearest garage for their inspection. BE PREPARED to switch off the engine should an unusual noise be heard.

Engine mechanical failure

Possible fault

Bearings worn, broken piston or ring, broken or burnt valve, blown gasket.

Check and Remedy

1 A blown gasket usually develops over a period of time so the fault should have been located earlier.
2 As a cylinder head gasket begins to fail oil sometimes finds its way into the cooling system or bubbles rise in the water. Conversely water may be found in the sump and will be noticed by a rise in oil level and water on the dipstick. If a gasket is suspect seek the services of the local garage.
3 In the case of a broken piston or connecting rod the engine will stop usually with a considerable amount of noise. The car will have to be towed to the garage for engine repairs.
4 Worn main bearings emit a heavy dull thudding noise especially when the engine is pulling under load or accelerating. With a worn big end the noise is somewhat lighter but still a metallic thud or knock. It is reduced if the spark plug lead is detached on the particular cylinder/ crankshaft journal.
5 Leave the plug lead detached. Carefully drive the car to the garage for engine repairs.

Car at rest, engine running and it is impossible to engage a gear without noise

---

Possible cause

The clutch is not disengaging correctly when the pedal is depressed.

Check and Remedy

1 With engine stationary move the selector lever to the neutral position and depress the clutch pedal by hand. Note the amount of free movement before any increased resistance is felt. It will probably be found the free movement is excessive (over 1 inch) so that the pedal movement does not free the clutch plate.
2 Adjust the clutch linkage (when possible) so that the free movement is that recommended by the manufacturer.
3 If this does not cure the trouble check that the hydraulic system reservoir (when fitted), is full of fluid and there is no air in the system. Bleed the system as necessary. Should this not cure the trouble either the hydraulic seals have failed or the clutch requires renewal.

Car at rest, engine running any gear selected, clutch engaged and when engine speed raised to drive clutch slip occurs

---

Possible cause

Clutch not engaging properly and is slipping, oil on the friction linings.

Check and Remedy

1 With engine stationary move the selector lever to the neutral position and depress the clutch pedal by hand, note the amount of free movement before any increased resistance is felt. It will probably be found that there is no free movement so that the pedal movement does not engage the clutch plate.
2 Adjust the clutch linkage (when possible) so that the free movement is to that recommended

by the manufacturer.

3 If this does not cure the trouble then it may be due to oil on the clutch lining, a worn rear engine bearing or seal or gearbox front bearing seal being defective.

4 If an aperture exists in the clutch bell housing wash out the clutch with carbon tetrachloride. This is found in many car type fire extinguishers and should enable the car to be driven home for repair. Keep the clutch pedal depressed whilst the liquid is squirted in.

5 Where the clutch is operated hydraulically it is possible for a seal to fail causing loss of control. Try opening and closing the slave cylinder bleed screw to relieve any pressure build up.

Transmission mechanical failure

Possible cause

Defective clutch, damaged gear teeth in gearbox or final drive. Broken half shaft.

Check and Remedy

If complete loss of drive is encountered it is best to seek expert advice as in some cases the car will have to be raised at the rear and towed or recovered on a trailer.

Brake failure

Possible cause

Excessive use of brake pedal causing overheating and brake fade. Hydraulic fluid leak.

Check and Remedy

Stop the car and if the brakes have overheated allow to cool down. If too hot, linings begin to smoke and begin to burn.

If the brakes suddenly fail stop the car using the best means possible without damage.

Check the level of hydraulic fluid in the reservoir and if empty check for signs of a leak at the pipes, flexible hoses, unions, master or wheel cylinders.

Do not attempt to drive the car without brakes but seek garage assistance.

Metric conversion tables

Inches	Millimetres	Inches	Millimetres
0.001	0.0254	0.1	2.54
0.002	0.0508	0.2	5.08
0.003	0.0762	0.3	7.62
0.004	0.1016	0.4	10.16
0.005	0.1270	0.5	12.70
0.006	0.1524	0.6	15.24
0.007	0.1778	0.7	17.78
0.008	0.2032	0.8	20.32
0.009	0.2286	0.9	22.96
0.01	0.254	1.0	25.4
0.02	0.508	2.0	50.8
0.03	0.762	3.0	76.2
0.04	1.016	4.0	101.6
0.05	1.270	5.0	127.0
0.06	1.524	6.0	152.4
0.07	1.778	7.0	177.8
0.08	2.032	8.0	203.2
0.09	2.286	9.0	228.6
		10.0	254.0

Inches	Decimals	Millimetres
1/64	0.0156	0.3969
1/32	0.0313	0.7937
1/16	0.0625	1.5875
1/8	0.125	3.1750
3/16	0.1875	4.7625
1/4	0.25	6.3500
5/16	0.3125	7.9375
3/8	0.375	9.5250
7/16	0.4375	11.1125
1/2	0.5	12.7000
9/16	0.5625	14.2875
5/8	0.625	15.8750
11/16	0.6875	17.4625
3/4	0.75	19.0500
13/16	0.8125	20.6375
7/8	0.875	22.2250
15/16	0.9375	23.8125

Torque Wrench Settings

lb ft	Kg m	Kg m	lb ft
1	0.138	1	7.233
2	0.276	2	14.466
3	0.414	3	21.699
4	0.553	4	28.932
5	0.691	5	36.165
6	0.829	6	43.398
7	0.967	7	50.631
8	1.106	8	57.864
9	1.244	9	65.097
10	1.382	10	72.330
20	2.765	20	144.660
30	4.147	30	216.990

Distance

Miles	Kilometres	Kilometres	Miles
1	1.61	1	0.62
2	3.22	2	1.24
3	4.83	3	1.86
4	6.44	4	2.49
5	8.05	5	3.11
6	9.66	6	3.73
7	11.27	7	4.35
8	12.88	8	4.97
9	14.48	9	5.59
10	16.09	10	6.21
20	32.19	20	12.43
30	48.28	30	18.64
40	64.37	40	24.85
50	80.47	50	31.07
60	96.56	60	37.28
70	112.65	70	43.50
80	128.75	80	49.71
90	144.84	90	55.92
100	160.93	100	62.14

Capacities

Pints	Litres	Litres	Pints	Gallons	Litres	Litres	Gallons
1	0.57	1	1.76	1	4.55	1	0.22
2	1.14	2	3.52	2	0.09	2	0.44
3	1.70	3	5.28	3	13.64	3	0.66
4	2.27	4	7.04	4	18.18	4	0.88
5	2.84	5	8.80	5	22.73	5	1.10
6	3.41	6	10.56	6	27.28	6	1.32
7	3.98	7	12.32	7	31.82	7	1.54
8	4.55	8	14.08	8	36.37	8	1.76
9	5.11	9	15.841	9	40.91	9	1.98
10	5.58	10	17.60	10	45.46	10	2.20
11	6.25	11	19.36	11	50.01	20	4.40
12	6.82	12	21.12	12	54.56	30	6.60

Tyre Pressures

lb/sq in	Kg/sq cm	Kg/sq cm	lb/sq in
1	0.07	1	14.22
2	0.14	2	28.50
3	0.21	3	42.67
4	0.28	4	56.89
5	0.35	5	71.12
6	0.42	6	85.34
7	0.49	7	99.56
8	0.56	8	113.79
9	0.63	9	128.00
10	0.70	10	142.23
20	1.41	20	284.47
30	2.11	30	426.70

Castrol at your service

Description of grades

Castrol Engine Oils

The highly-stressed modern engine makes demands on its lubricant that were undreamed of a few years ago. Castrol engine oils are designed to meet those demands. They are the product of the best lubricant research, and are an outstanding example of advanced lubricating technology.

Castrol GTX
An ultra high performance motor oil, which generously protects engines at the extreme limits of performance, and combines both good cold starting with oil consumption control. Approved by leading car manufacturers and recommended for all passenger cars in all seasons.

Castrol XL 20/50
Containing liquid tungsten, well suited to the majority of conditions, giving good oil consumption control in both new and old cars.

Castrolite (10W/30)
This is the lightest multigrade oil of the range of Castrol motor oils containing liquid tungsten. It is best suited to ensure easy winter starting for those car models whose manufacturers specify lighter weight oils.

Castrol Grand Prix
An SAE 50 oil for use where a heavy, full-bodied lubricant is required.

Castrol TT Two-stroke Oil
A high quality, clean burning oil for all two-stroke engines. Contains anti-corrosion, anti-scuff and anti-port blocking additives. It has good low temperature flow characteristics and has excellent miscibility with petrol. It has been specifically formulated for use in all two-stroke engines in cars, motorcycles (in particular the Japanese models fitted with Autolube, Posiforce and Superlube lubricating systems), and horticultural machines.

Castrol CR (Multi-grade)
A high quality engine oil of the SAE 20W/30 multi-grade type suited to mixed fleet operations.

Castrol CRI 10, 20, 30
Primarily for diesel engines, a range of heavily fortified, fully detergent oils, covering the requirements of DEF 2101-D and Supplement 1 specifications.

Castrol CRB 20, 30
Primarily for diesel engines, heavily fortified, fully detergent oils, covering the requirements of MIL-L-2104B.

Castrol R40
Designed and developed for highly stressed racing engines. Castrol 'R' should not be mixed with any other oil nor with any other grade of Castrol.

Castrol Horticultural oil
An SAE 30 lubricant especially produced for use in all lawn and garden machinery with four-stroke engines.

Castrol Gear Oils

Castrol Hypoy (90 EP)
A light-bodied powerful extreme pressure gear oil for use in hypoid rear axles and in some gearboxes.

Castrol Hypoy Light (EP 80W)
A very light-bodied powerful extreme pressure gear oil for use in hypoid rear axles in cold climates and in some gearboxes.

Castrol Hypoy B (90 EP)
A light-bodied powerful extreme pressure gear oil that complies with the requirements of the MIL-L-2105B specification, for use in certain gearboxes and rear axles.

Castrol Hi-Press (140 EP)
A heavy-bodied extreme pressure gear oil for use in spiral bevel rear axles and some gearboxes.

Castrol ST (90)
A light-bodied gear oil with fortifying additives.

Castrol D (140)
A heavy full-bodied gear oil with fortifying additives.

Castrol Thio-Hypoy FD (90 EP)
A light-bodied powerful extreme pressure gear oil. This is a special oil for running-in certain hypoid gears.

Automatic Transmission Fluids

Castrol TQF
Approved for use in all Borg-Warner Automatic Transmission Units. Castrol TQF also meets Ford specification M2C 33F.

Castrol TQ Dexron ®
Complies with the requirements of Dexron ® Automatic Transmission Fluids as laid down by General Motors Corporation.

Castrol Greases

Castrol LM
A multi-purpose high melting point lithium based grease approved for most automotive applications including chassis and wheel bearing lubrication.

Castrol MS3
A high melting point lithium based grease containing molybdenum disulphide.

Castrol BNS
A high melting point grease for use where recommended by certain manufacturers in front wheel bearings when disc brakes are fitted.

Castrol CL
A semi-fluid calcium based grease, which is both waterproof and adhesive, intended for chassis lubrication.

Castrol Medium
A medium consistency calcium based grease.

Castrol Heavy
A heavy consistency calcium based grease.

Castrol PH
A white grease for plunger housings and other moving parts on brake mechanisms. *(It must NOT be allowed to come into contact with brake fluid when applied to the moving parts of hydraulic brakes).*

Castrol Graphited Grease
A graphited grease for the lubrication of transmission chains.

Castrol Water Pump
A specially formulated grease for automotive water pumps

Castrol Under-Water Grease
A grease for the under-water gears of outboard motors.

Speciality Products

Castrol Girling Universal Brake & Clutch Fluid
Specially developed in conjunction with Girling Limited, a high quality product with a boiling point in excess of 550º F. *The Universal Fluid* which meets the severest demands of modern motoring in all brake and clutch systems.*
* except Citroen and special mineral fluid systems.

Castrol Girling Damper Oil Thin
The oil for Girling piston type hydraulic dampers.

Castrol LHS 2
A vegetable-based fluid approved by Citroen Cars Ltd., for the hydraulic systems of all models DS, DW, ID, Safari and Convertible produced from 1955 to September 1966, where the hydraulic reservoirs and components of these cars are not painted green; the fluid itself is red.

Castrol LHM
This is a mineral-based fluid approved by Citroen Cars Ltd. for models DS, ID, Safari and Convertible produced from September 1966. Castrol LHM is green in colour, the hydraulic reservoirs and components of the models mentioned are also painted green.
Note: *It is important that the fluid used for replenishing the system is kept clean and free from contamination. On no account mix Castrol LHS 2 or Castrol LHM with any other oil or fluid.*

Castrol Shockol
A light viscosity oil for use in some piston type shock absorbers and in some hydraulic systems employing synthetic rubber seals. It must not be used in braking systems.

Castrol Solvent Flushing Oil
A light-bodied solvent oil, designed for flushing engines, rear axles, gearboxes and gearcasings.

Everyman Oil

A light-bodied machine oil containing anti-corrosion additives for both general use and cycle lubrication.

Castrol Anti-Freeze

Contains anti-corrosion additives with ethylene glycol. Recommended for the cooling systems of all petrol and diesel engines.

Castrol KLIX

A pleasantly odoured antiseptic hand cleanser gel. Will remove from the skin, oil, grease, new paint, glue, dirt, household grease and beach tar. Safe for all types of skin.

Castrol Pack Availability

Grades Engine & Gear Oils	Drums	Screw-Top Tins			Strip-Seal Pack		Handi-Pack
	5 gall	1 gal	1 qt	1 pt	1 qt	1 pt	1 pt
Castrol GTX	*	*			*	*	*
Castrol XL	*	*			*	*	*
Castrolite	*	*			*	*	
Castrol Grand Prix	*	*	*				
Castrol TT Two-Stroke Oil	*	*			1 pt Ratio Pack		
Castrol CR (Multi-Grade)	*						
Castrol CRI 10, 20, 30	*	*	*	*			
Castrol CRB 20, 30	*						
Castrol R40	*	*	*				
Castrol Horticultural Oil (as per TT)	*	*			1 pt Ratio Pack		
Castrol Hypoy	*	*	*				*
Castrol Hypoy Light	*	*	*				*
Castrol Hypoy B	*						*
Castrol Hi-Press	*	*	*				*
Castrol ST	*	*	*				*
Castrol D	*	*	*				
Castrol Thio-Hypoy FD	*						
Castrol TQF	*	*	*				*
Castrol TQ Dexron ©	*	*	*				*

Greases	28 lb. Bucket	7 lb. Tin	1 lb. Tin	Speciality Products	Available in
Castrol LM		*	*	Castrol Girling Universal Brake & Clutch Fluid	25 litre drum, 5 litre, 1 litre, 500 ml.,
Castrol MS3		*	*	Castrol Girling Brake & Clutch Fluid Crimson	250 ml., tins.
Castrol BNS				Castrol Girling Damper Oil Thin	1 gall and 1 pt tins
Castrol CL		*	*	Castrol LHS2	1 qt tin
				Castrol LHM	1 litre tin
Castrol Medium		*	*	Castrol Shockol	1 qt tin
				Castrol Solvent Flushing Oil	1 gall and 1 qt tins
Castrol Heavy		*	*	Everyman Oil	250 ml. & 125 ml., tins
Castrol PH				Castrol Anti-Freeze	5 gall drum, 1 gall tin 1 qt and 1 pt strip seal cans
Castrol Graphited					
Castrol Water Pump				Castrol Klix Hand Cleanser	7 oz. tube
Castrol Under Water					

** Pushdown Tins*

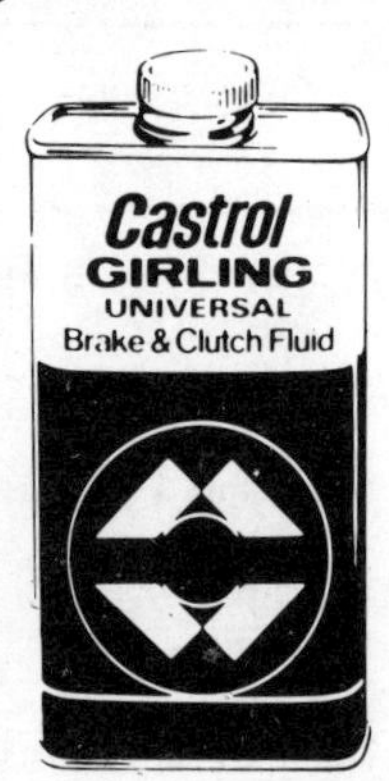
Castrol
GIRLING
UNIVERSAL
Brake & Clutch Fluid

Castrol
XL
THE EXTRA STRENGTH
20
50

Castrol
Automatic
Transmission Fluid
TQ (DEXRON)

Castrol
MOTOR OIL
CRI 30
Castrol

Castrol
LM
High melting point
Avoid overpacking bearing
GREASE
Castrol

Castrol
HYPOY B
EP 90

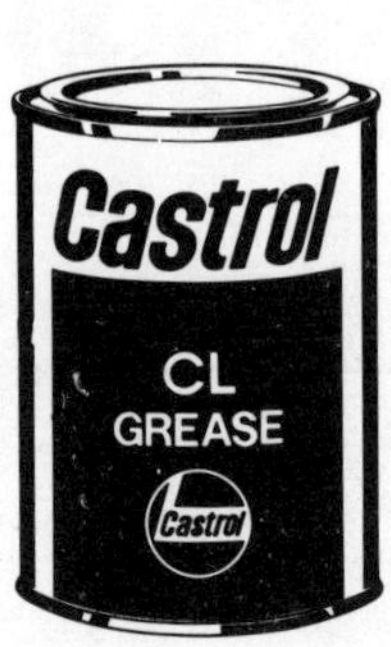
Castrol
CL
GREASE
Castrol

Castrol
GTX
HIGH PERFORMANCE MOTOR OIL
Castrol

CASTROL
D 140
gear oil
HANDI-PACK
DISPENSER
CASTROL LIMITED LONDON

Castrol
Automatic
Transmission Fluid
TQF

Castrol
HYPOY LIGHT
EP 80W
gear oil

CASTROLITE
10-30 with LIQUID TUNGSTEN

Castrol
MS3
(High melting point)
Containing Molybdenum Disulphide
GREASE
Castrol

Castrol
ANTI-FREEZE
GREASE
Castrol

CASTROL XL
20W-50
motor oil
HANDI-PACK
DISPENSER
CASTROL LIMITED LONDON

Castrol
BNS
(High melting point)
GREASE
Castrol